AQA GCSE Spanish
Higher
Vocabulary Book

Published by Pearson Education Limited, 80 Strand, London, WC2R 0RL
www.pearsonschoolsandfecolleges.co.uk
Text © Pearson Education Limited 2017
Editorial management by Gwladys Rushworth for Haremi
Edited by Ruth Manteca
Typeset by York Publishing Solutions Pvt. Ltd.
Cover image: Shutterstock.com: David Pereiras
Cover © Pearson Education Limited 2017

Written by Penny Fisher

First published 2017
10 9 8 7

British Library Cataloguing in Publication Data
A catalogue record for this book is available from the British Library.
ISBN 978 1 292 13244 0

Copyright notice
All rights reserved. No part of this publication may be reproduced in any form or by any means (including photocopying or storing it in any medium by electronic means and whether or not transiently or incidentally to some other use of this publication) without the written permission of the copyright owner, except in accordance with the provisions of the Copyright, Design and Patents Act 1988 or under the terms of a license issued by the Copyright Licensing Agency, Barnard's Inn, 86 Fetter Lane, London EC4A 1EN (www.cla.co.uk). Applications for the copyright owner's written permission should be addressed to the publisher.

Printed in the UK by Ashford Colour Press

Contenidos

High-frequency words 4

Módulo 1
Words I should know for speaking and writing activities 12
Extra words I should know for reading and listening activities 15

Módulo 2
Words I should know for speaking and writing activities 16
Extra words I should know for reading and listening activities 19

Módulo 3
Words I should know for speaking and writing activities 20
Extra words I should know for reading and listening activities 23

Módulo 4
Words I should know for speaking and writing activities 24
Extra words I should know for reading and listening activities 27

Módulo 5
Words I should know for speaking and writing activities 28
Extra words I should know for reading and listening activities 32

Módulo 6
Words I should know for speaking and writing activities 33
Extra words I should know for reading and listening activities 36

Módulo 7
Words I should know for speaking and writing activities 37
Extra words I should know for reading and listening activities 41

Módulo 8
Words I should know for speaking and writing activities 42
Extra words I should know for reading and listening activities 46

High-frequency words

Common verbs

alcanzar	to reach
abrir	to open
cerrar	to close
comenzar	to begin
continuar	to continue
corregir	to correct
dar	to give
dejar de	to stop (doing something)
echar	to throw
empezar	to begin
estar equivocado/a	to make a mistake / to be wrong
hacer	to do / to make
ir	to go
irse	to go away / to leave
mentir	to tell a lie
necesitar	to need
permitir	to allow
poner	to put
ponerse a	to start doing something
prohibir	to forbid / to ban
seguir	to continue / to follow
tener	to have / to own
tener razón	to be right

Had a look ☐ **Nearly there** ☐ **Nailed it** ☐

acabar de + infinitive	to have just (done something)
deber	must / to have to
estar	to be
hace(n) falta	to need / to be necessary
hacerse	to become
hay	there is / there are
hay que	one must / one has to
ir a + infinitive	(to be) going to (do something)
poder	to be able / can
ser	to be
soler + infinitive	to regularly do (something)
tener que + infinitive	to have to do (something)
volver a + infinitive	to do (something) again
volverse	to become

Had a look ☐ **Nearly there** ☐ **Nailed it** ☐

bastar	to be enough
durar	to last
estar situado/a	to be situated
encontrarse	to be situated
hace (+ time) …	it's been …
medir	to measure
mojar(se)	to get wet
ocurrir	to happen
pasar	to happen / to go through / to spend (time)
pesar	to weigh
tener (calor / frío)	to feel (hot / cold)
tener lugar	to take place
tener prisa	to be in a hurry
valer la pena	to be worth the trouble

Had a look ☐ **Nearly there** ☐ **Nailed it** ☐

adorar	to adore / to love
alegrar	to cheer up
alegrarse (de)	to be happy about
apreciar	to appreciate
aprovechar	to make the most
aprovecharse (de)	to take advantage (of)
desear	to wish
disfrutar	to enjoy
divertirse	to have a good time
encantar	to delight
estar a favor de	to be in favour of
estar de acuerdo	to agree
pasarlo bien / mal	to have a good / bad time
querer	to want / to love
sentir(se)	to feel

Had a look ☐ **Nearly there** ☐ **Nailed it** ☐

creer	to believe
darse cuenta (de)	to realise
decidir	to decide
decir	to say
dudar	to doubt
esperar	to hope
opinar	to think / to give an opinion
parecer	to seem
pensar	to think
ponerse de acuerdo	to agree
preferir	to prefer
quedar en	to agree
querer decir	to mean
reconocer	to recognise
saber	to know (a fact / how to do something)
tener razón	to be right

Had a look ☐ **Nearly there** ☐ **Nailed it** ☐

aburrirse	to get bored
decepcionar	to disappoint
dar igual	to be all the same / to make no difference
estar en contra	to be against
estar harto/a de	to be fed up with
fastidiar	to annoy / to bother
odiar	to hate

Had a look ☐ **Nearly there** ☐ **Nailed it** ☐

High-frequency words

Common adjectives

afortunado/a	lucky	distinto/a	different
agradable	pleasant	duro/a	hard
alucinante	amazing	equivocado/a	wrong
bonito/a	pretty	fácil	easy
bueno/a	good	gratis / gratuito/a	free (of charge)
divertido/a	amusing / entertaining	libre	free / unoccupied
emocionante	exciting / thrilling / moving	lento/a	slow
encantador(a)	charming	mediano/a	medium
entretenido/a	entertaining / amusing	ocupado/a	engaged / occupied
espléndido/a	fantastic / great / terrific	profundo/a	deep / profound
estupendo/a	fantastic / marvellous	raro/a	strange / rare
fenomenal	great / fantastic	seguro/a	safe / certain / self-assured
genial	brilliant / great	sencillo/a	simple / plain / straightforward
guay	cool	sorprendido/a	surprised
hermoso/a	beautiful	tranquilo/a	peaceful / quiet
maravilloso/a	marvellous	único/a	unique / only / single
impresionante	impressive / striking	útil	useful
increíble	incredible		
precioso/a	precious / beautiful		

Had a look ☐   Nearly there ☐   Nailed it ☐

aburrido/a	boring / bored		
decepcionado/a	disappointed		
decepcionante	disappointing		
desagradable	unpleasant		
fatal	awful / fatal		
horroroso/a	horrible		
inseguro	unsafe / uncertain / insecure		
inútil	useless		
malo/a	bad		

Had a look ☐   Nearly there ☐   Nailed it ☐

Common adverbs

afortunadamente	fortunately
bien	well
casi	almost
deprisa	quickly
desafortunadamente	unfortunately
desgraciadamente	unfortunately
especialmente	especially
inmediatamente	immediately
mal	badly
más	more
no obstante	nevertheless
por suerte	fortunately
quizás / quizá	perhaps
rápidamente	quickly
realmente	really
recientemente	recently
sin embargo	nevertheless
sobre todo	especially

Had a look ☐   Nearly there ☐   Nailed it ☐

abierto/a	open
alto/a	tall / high
ancho/a	wide
antiguo/a	old
bajo/a	low / short
cerrado/a	closed
delgado/a	slim / thin
estrecho/a	narrow
feo/a	ugly
gordo/a	fat
grueso/a	thick
lleno/a	full
nuevo/a	new
tonto/a	silly
vacío/a	empty
viejo/a	old

Had a look ☐   Nearly there ☐   Nailed it ☐

Prepositions

a	to / at
de	from / of
en	in
hacia	towards
hasta	until
para	for
por	through / by / in / for / per
según	according to
sin	without

Had a look ☐   Nearly there ☐   Nailed it ☐

apropiado/a	correct / appropriate
barato/a	cheap
caro/a	expensive
cierto/a	certain / sure / true

Connectives

además	moreover / besides
aparte de	apart from
claro que	of course

5

High-frequency words

dado que	given that	pues	then / since
es decir	in other words / that is to say	si	if
		sin embargo	however
por un lado ... por otro lado	on the one hand ... on the other hand	tal vez	maybe / perhaps
		también	also
por una parte ... por otra parte	on the one hand ... on the other hand	ya que	as / since
sin duda	obviously / certainly / undoubtedly		

Had a look ☐ Nearly there ☐ Nailed it ☐

Had a look ☐ Nearly there ☐ Nailed it ☐

Negatives

jamás	never
ni ... ni	neither ... nor
nada	nothing
nadie	nobody
ninguno/a	none / no one / any / no
nunca	never
sino	but / except
tampoco	neither / not ... either ...
ya no	not any more

Question words

¿(a)dónde?	where?
¿cómo?	how?
¿cuál(es)?	which?
¿cuándo?	when?
¿cuánto/a?	how much?
¿cuántos/as ...?	how many?
¿de dónde?	where from?
¿de quién?	whose?
¿por dónde?	through where?
¿por qué?	why?
¿qué?	what?
¿quién?	who?

Had a look ☐ Nearly there ☐ Nailed it ☐

Had a look ☐ Nearly there ☐ Nailed it ☐

Comparisons / Superlatives

bastante	sufficient / enough / quite
demasiado/a	too / too much
igual que	same as
más (que)	more (than)
mayor	main / major / larger / bigger / greater
la mayoría	most / majority
mejor	better / best
menor	smaller / less / least
menos (que)	less (than)
mismo/a	same
muy	very
parecido/a a	like / similar to
peor	worse / worst
poco (ruidoso)	not very (noisy)
tan ... como	as ... as
tanto/a ... como	as much ... as

¿a qué hora?	at what time?
¿cuánto cuesta(n)?	how much does it / do they cost?
¿cuánto es?	how much is it?
¿cuánto vale(n)?	how much does it / do they cost?
¿cuántos años tiene(s)?	how old are you?
¿de qué color?	what colour?
¿para / por cuánto tiempo?	for how long?
¿qué día?	what day?
¿qué fecha?	what date?
¿qué hora es?	what time is it?

Had a look ☐ Nearly there ☐ Nailed it ☐

Time expressions

a la una	at one o'clock
a las dos, etc.	at two o'clock, etc.
y cinco, etc.	five past, etc.
y cuarto	quarter past
y media	half past
menos cuarto	quarter to
menos diez, etc.	ten to, etc.
de la mañana	in the morning
de la tarde	in the afternoon / in the evening
es la una	it's one o'clock
son las dos, etc.	it's two o'clock, etc.
la hora	hour
el minuto	minute
la medianoche	midnight
el mediodía	noon

Had a look ☐ Nearly there ☐ Nailed it ☐

Conjunctions

a pesar de	in spite of / despite
así que	so / therefore
aun (cuando)	even (if)
aunque	although / (even) though
como	as / since
cuando	when
incluso	even
mientras (que)	while / meanwhile
o/u	or
pero	but
por eso	for that reason / therefore
por lo tanto	therefore
porque	because

Had a look ☐ Nearly there ☐ Nailed it ☐

High-frequency words

el año	year
anoche	last night
ayer	yesterday
el día	day
el fin de semana	weekend
el mes	month
la estación	season
esta noche	tonight
hoy	today
la fecha	date
la mañana	morning
la noche	night
la semana	week
la tarde	afternoon / evening
mañana	tomorrow
pasado mañana	day after tomorrow
quince días	fortnight
el rato	while / short time
el pasado	past
el porvenir	future

Had a look ☐ Nearly there ☐ Nailed it ☐

Days, months and seasons of the year

lunes	Monday
martes	Tuesday
miércoles	Wednesday
jueves	Thursday
viernes	Friday
sábado	Saturday
domingo	Sunday
(el) lunes	(on) Monday
(el) lunes por la mañana	(on) Monday morning
(el) lunes por la tarde	(on) Monday evening
los lunes	on Mondays
cada lunes	every Monday

Had a look ☐ Nearly there ☐ Nailed it ☐

enero	January
febrero	February
marzo	March
abril	April
mayo	May
junio	June
julio	July
agosto	August
septiembre	September
octubre	October
noviembre	November
diciembre	December

Had a look ☐ Nearly there ☐ Nailed it ☐

la primavera	spring
el verano	summer
el otoño	autumn
el invierno	winter

Had a look ☐ Nearly there ☐ Nailed it ☐

Frequency expressions

a diario	daily / everyday
a eso de …	at about …
a mediados de …	around the middle of …
a menudo	often
a partir de	from
a veces	sometimes
ahora	now / nowadays
al mismo tiempo	at the same time
algunas veces	sometimes
antes (de)	before
cada (…) días / horas	every (…) days / hours
de vez en cuando	now and then / from time to time
dentro de (…) días / horas	within (…) days / hours
desde / desde hace	since
después (de)	after / afterwards
durante	during
en seguida / enseguida	straightaway
entonces	then
luego	then / afterwards
mientras tanto	meanwhile

Had a look ☐ Nearly there ☐ Nailed it ☐

de momento	at the moment / right now
de nuevo	again
otra vez	again
de repente	suddenly
(por) mucho tiempo	(for) a long time
pocas veces	seldom / a few times
por fin	at last
al principio	at the beginning
pronto	soon
próximo/a	next
que viene (el mes, etc.)	next (month, etc.)
siempre	always
siguiente	next / following
sobre	on / around
tarde	late
temprano	early
todos/as (las semanas / los días / meses)	every (week / day / month)
todavía	still / yet
último/a	last
una vez (dos / tres veces, etc.)	once (twice / three times, etc.)
ya	already

Had a look ☐ Nearly there ☐ Nailed it ☐

Location and distance

abajo (de)	under / below
afuera (de)	outside
ahí	there
allá	over there
allí	over there

7

High-frequency words

atrás	behind	diecisiete	17
delante (de)	in front of	dieciocho	18
detrás (de)	behind	diecinueve	19
cerca (de)	near	veinte	20

Had a look ☐ Nearly there ☐ Nailed it ☐

enfrente (de)	opposite		
entre	between	veintiuno	21
a la derecha / izquierda	on the / to the right / left	veintidós	22
a mano derecha / izquierda	on the right / left	veintitrés	23
		veinticuatro	24
a un paso (de)	a few steps away	veinticinco	25
al final (de)	at the end of	veintiséis	26
al lado (de)	next to	veintisiete	27
en la esquina	on the corner	veintiocho	28
todo recto	straight on / ahead	veintinueve	29
		treinta	30

Had a look ☐ Nearly there ☐ Nailed it ☐

Had a look ☐ Nearly there ☐ Nailed it ☐

alrededor (de)	around		
aquí	here	cuarenta	40
arriba (de)	above / on top (of)	cincuenta	50
cercano/a	nearby	sesenta	60
contra	against	setenta	70
debajo (de)	under	ochenta	80
dentro (de)	inside	noventa	90
en el medio (de)	in the middle of	cien(to)	100
en / por todas partes	everywhere	ciento uno/a	101
en las afueras	in the outskirts	doscientos/as	200
encima (de)	above / on top / overhead	mil	1,000
		mil cien(to)	1,100
el este	east	dos mil	2,000
en el / al fondo	at the back / at the bottom	(un) millón (de)	1,000,000
fuera (de)	outside		

Had a look ☐ Nearly there ☐ Nailed it ☐

lejos (de)	far (from)		
el lugar	place	primer / primero/a	first
el norte	north	segundo/a	second
el oeste	west	tercer / tercero/a	third
el sitio	place	cuarto/a	fourth
el sur	south	quinto/a	fifth

Had a look ☐ Nearly there ☐ Nailed it ☐

Numbers

		sexto/a	sixth
uno	1	séptimo/a	seventh
dos	2	octavo/a	eighth
tres	3	noveno/a	ninth
cuatro	4	décimo/a	tenth

Had a look ☐ Nearly there ☐ Nailed it ☐

cinco	5		
seis	6	mil novecientos noventa y cinco	1995
siete	7		
ocho	8	dos mil diecisiete	2017
nueve	9	(una) docena	dozen
diez	10	el número	number
once	11	un par	pair / couple
doce	12	unos/as (diez)	about (10)
trece	13		
catorce	14		
quince	15		
dieciséis	16		

Had a look ☐ Nearly there ☐ Nailed it ☐

High-frequency words

Colours
amarillo/a	yellow
azul	blue
blanco/a	white
castaño/a	chestnut brown
claro/a	light
el color	colour
gris	grey
marrón	brown
morado/a / violeta	purple / violet
moreno/a	dark (hair / skin)
naranja	orange
negro	black
oscuro/a	dark
pálido/a	pale
rojo/a	red
rosa / rosado/a	pink
rubio/a	fair (hair / skin)
verde	green
vivo/a	vivid / bright

Had a look ☐ **Nearly there** ☐ **Nailed it** ☐

Weather
el cielo	sky
el clima	climate
el chubasco	shower
la lluvia	rain
la niebla	fog
la nieve	snow
la nube	cloud
el pronóstico	forecast
el relámpago	lightning
el grado	degree
el hielo	ice
el tiempo	weather
la tormenta	storm
el trueno	thunder
el viento	wind

Had a look ☐ **Nearly there** ☐ **Nailed it** ☐

caliente	hot
caluroso	hot / warm
despejado	clear (skies)
estable	stable / steady / unchanged
fresco	fresh
húmedo	humid
nublado / nuboso	cloudy
seco	dry
la sombra	shade / shadow
templado	mild / temperate
tormentoso	stormy
buen / mal tiempo	good / bad weather
hacer (frío / calor / etc.)	to be (cold / hot / etc.)
helar	to freeze
llover	to rain
mojar(se)	to get wet
nevar	to snow
tener (calor / frío)	to feel (hot / cold)

Had a look ☐ **Nearly there** ☐ **Nailed it** ☐

Weights, measures and containers
la altura	height
el ancho / la anchura	width
la bolsa	bag
el bote	jar
la caja	box
la cantidad	quantity
el cartón	carton
un cuarto	quarter
la lata	tin
la medida	measure
medio	half
la mitad	half
el pedazo	piece
el peso	weight
un poco	little
la ración	portion
la talla	size (clothes)
el tamaño	size
el trozo	piece

Had a look ☐ **Nearly there** ☐ **Nailed it** ☐

Countries and continents
Alemania	Germany
Austria	Austria
Bélgica	Belgium
Dinamarca	Denmark
Escocia	Scotland
España	Spain
Francia	France
Gran Bretaña	Great Britain
Grecia	Greece
Holanda	Holland
Inglaterra	England
Irlanda	Ireland
Italia	Italy
(País de) Gales	Wales
Países Bajos	Netherlands
Reino Unido	United Kingdom
Suecia	Sweden
Suiza	Switzerland
Turquía	Turkey

Had a look ☐ **Nearly there** ☐ **Nailed it** ☐

Argentina	Argentina
Brasil	Brazil
Estados Unidos	United States
India	India
México	Mexico
Pakistán	Pakistan

High-frequency words

Perú	Peru
Rusia	Russia

Had a look ☐ **Nearly there** ☐ **Nailed it** ☐

África	Africa
América del Norte / Norteamérica	North America
América del Sur / Sudamérica	South America
América Latina / Latinoamérica	Latin America
Asia	Asia
Australia	Australia
Europa	Europe

Had a look ☐ **Nearly there** ☐ **Nailed it** ☐

Nationalities

alemán/alemana	German
austriaco/a	Austrian
belga	Belgian
británico/a	British
danés/danesa	Danish
escocés/escocesa	Scottish
español/a	Spanish
europeo/a	European
francés/francesa	French
galés/galesa	Welsh
griego/a	Greek
holandés/holandesa	Dutch
inglés/inglesa	English
irlandés/irlandesa	Irish
italiano/a	Italian
sueco/a	Swedish
suizo/a	Swiss
turco/a	Turkish

Had a look ☐ **Nearly there** ☐ **Nailed it** ☐

americano/a	American
argentino/a	Argentinian
boliviano/a	Bolivian
brasileño/a	Brazilian
chileno/a	Chilean
chino/a	Chinese
colombiano/a	Colombian
ecuatoriano/a	Ecuadorean
indio/a	Indian
italiano/a	Italian
japonés/japonesa	Japanese
mexicano/a	Mexican
pakistaní	Pakistani
peruano/a	Peruvian
ruso/a	Russian
venezolano/a	Venezuelan

Had a look ☐ **Nearly there** ☐ **Nailed it** ☐

Areas, mountains and seas

Andalucía	Andalusia
Aragón	Aragon
el canal de la Mancha	the English Channel
Castilla	Castile
Cataluña	Catalonia
comunidades autónomas	autonomous communities
Galicia	Galicia
el mar Cantábrico	Cantabrian Sea
el mar Mediterráneo	Mediterranean Sea
el océano Atlántico	Atlantic Ocean
(el) País Vasco	(the) Basque Country
los Pirineos	the Pyrenees
La Rioja	Rioja

Had a look ☐ **Nearly there** ☐ **Nailed it** ☐

Materials

el algodón	cotton
la cerámica	pottery
el cristal	glass / crystal
el cuero	leather
la lana	wool
la madera	wood
el oro	gold
el papel	paper
la piel	leather / skin
la plata	silver
la seda	silk
la tela	fabric / material
el vidrio	glass

Had a look ☐ **Nearly there** ☐ **Nailed it** ☐

Greetings and exclamations

¿Cómo está(s)?	How are you?
¿De veras?	Really?
con permiso	excuse me
de nada	you're welcome / don't mention it
encantado/a	pleased to meet you
hasta el (lunes)	till / see you (Monday)
hasta luego	see you later
hasta mañana	see you tomorrow
hasta pronto	see you soon
lo siento	I'm sorry
mucho gusto	pleased to meet you
perdón	sorry
perdone	sorry
por favor	please
¡Que lo pase(s) bien!	Have a good time!
¿Qué hay?	What's happening? / What's the matter?
¿Qué pasa?	What's happening? / What's the matter?
¿Qué tal?	How are you? / How's …?
saludar	to greet / to say hello

High-frequency words

saludos	regards / greetings	de acuerdo	OK (I agree)
vale	OK	depende	it depends
		en mi opinión	in my opinion
		estoy bien	I'm fine

Had a look ☐ Nearly there ☐ Nailed it ☐

¡Basta ya!	That's enough!
¡Bienvenido/a!	Welcome!
¡Buen viaje!	Have a good trip!
¡Buena suerte!	Good luck!
¡Claro!	Of course!
¡Cuidado!	Careful! / Watch out!
¡Enhorabuena!	Congratulations!
¡Felices vacaciones!	Have a good holiday!
¡Felicidades!	Best wishes! / Congratulations!
¡Felicitaciones!	Congratulations!
¡Ojo!	Watch out! / Careful!
¡Qué (+ adjective)!	How …!
¡Qué (+ noun)!	What a …!
¡Que suerte!	What luck!
¡Qué va!	Come on! / Rubbish! / Nonsense!
¡Socorro!	Help!

gracias	thank you
he tenido bastante	I've had enough
me da igual	I don't mind
menos mal	just as well
mío/a	mine
no importa	it doesn't matter
otra vez	once again
por supuesto	of course
por si acaso	just in case
qué lástima / qué pena	what a shame
ten (informal) / tenga (formal)	there you are (informal / formal)

Had a look ☐ Nearly there ☐ Nailed it ☐

Other useful words

algo	something
alguien	someone
la cifra	figure
como	as / like
la cosa	thing
la desventaja	disadvantage
todo el mundo	everybody
todos	everybody
eso/a/os/as	that / those
esto/a/os/as	this / these

Had a look ☐ Nearly there ☐ Nailed it ☐

Language used in dialogues and messages

a la atención de	for the attention of
el auricular	receiver (telephone)
con relación a	further to / following
de momento	at the moment
en contacto con	in communication with
enviado/a por	sent by
escucho / dígame	I'm listening
espere	wait
hablando / al aparato / en la línea	on the line / speaking
le paso	I will put you through
llámame (informal) / llámeme (formal)	call me (informal / formal)
marcar el número	dial the number
el mensaje (de texto)	text message
el mensaje en el contestador	voice mail
no cuelgue	stay on the line
el número equivocado	wrong number
el prefijo	area code
el teléfono	telephone
el texto	text
el timbre / el tono	tone
vuelvo enseguida	I'll be right back

la falta	error
la forma	shape
la forma	way
la manera	way
el género	type / kind / sort
el tipo	type / kind / sort
el medio	middle
la mitad	half
no	no
el número	number
por ejemplo	for example
la razón	reason
señor	Mr
señora	Mrs
señorita	Miss
si	if
sí	yes
la ventaja	advantage
la verdad	truth

Had a look ☐ Nearly there ☐ Nailed it ☐

Had a look ☐ Nearly there ☐ Nailed it ☐

Other useful expressions

aquí lo tiene(s)	here you are
buena suerte	good luck
¿Cómo se escribe?	How do you spell that?
con (mucho) gusto / placer	with pleasure

11

Módulo 1 Palabras

Words I should know for speaking and writing activities

¿Dónde vives?	Where do you live?
Vivo en el …	I live in the …
norte / noreste / noroeste …	north / northeast / northwest …
sur / sureste / suroeste …	south / southeast / southwest …
este / oeste / centro …	east / west / centre …
de Inglaterra / Escocia	of England / Scotland
de Gales / Irlanda (del Norte)	of Wales / (Northern) Ireland

Had a look ☐ Nearly there ☐ Nailed it ☐

¿Qué haces en verano?	What do you do in summer?
En verano / invierno …	In summer / winter …
chateo en la red	I chat online
cocino para mi familia	I cook for my family
descargo canciones	I download songs
escribo correos	I write emails
hago natación / esquí / windsurf	I go swimming / skiing / windsurfing
hago una barbacoa	I have a barbecue
juego al baloncesto / fútbol	I play basketball / football
monto a caballo / en bici	I go horseriding / cycling
nado en el mar	I swim in the sea
salgo con mis amigos/as	I go out with my friends
toco la guitarra	I play the guitar
trabajo como voluntario/a	I work as a volunteer
veo la tele	I watch TV
voy al polideportivo / al parque / a un centro comercial	I go to the sports centre / to the park / to a shopping centre
voy de paseo	I go for a walk

Had a look ☐ Nearly there ☐ Nailed it ☐

¿Con qué frecuencia?	How often?
siempre	always
a menudo	often
todos los días	every day
a veces	sometimes
de vez en cuando	from time to time
una vez a la semana	once a week
dos o tres veces al año	two or three times a year
(casi) nunca	(almost) never

Had a look ☐ Nearly there ☐ Nailed it ☐

¿Qué tiempo hace?	What's the weather like?
Hace buen / mal tiempo.	It's good / bad weather.
Hace calor / frío / sol / viento.	It's hot / cold / sunny / windy.
Llueve / Nieva.	It's raining / snowing.
El tiempo es variable.	The weather is changeable.
El clima es caluroso / soleado.	The climate is hot / sunny.
Hay niebla / tormenta.	It's foggy / stormy.
Hay chubascos.	There are showers.
Está nublado.	It's cloudy.

Had a look ☐ Nearly there ☐ Nailed it ☐

¿Qué te gusta hacer?	What do you like doing?
Soy adicto/a a …	I'm addicted to …
Soy un(a) fanático/a de … ya que / dado que / puesto que …	I'm a … fan / fanatic … given that / since …
Prefiero …	I prefer …
Me gusta …	I like …
Me encanta / Me mola / Me chifla / Me flipa / Me apasiona …	I love …

Had a look ☐ Nearly there ☐ Nailed it ☐

No me gusta (nada) …	I don't like … (at all)
Odio …	I hate …
A (mi padre) le gusta …	(My dad) likes …
Nos encanta …	We love …
bucear	diving
estar al aire libre	being outdoors
estar en contacto con los amigos	being in touch with friends
hacer artes marciales	doing martial arts
hacer deportes acuáticos	doing water sports
ir al cine / a la pista de hielo	going to the cinema / ice rink
ir de compras	going shopping
leer (un montón de revistas)	reading (loads of magazines)
usar el ordenador	using the computer
ver películas	watching films
Prefiero veranear …	I prefer to spend the summer …
en el extranjero / en España	abroad / in Spain
en la costa / en el campo	on the coast / in the country
en la montaña / en la ciudad	in the mountains / in the city

Had a look ☐ Nearly there ☐ Nailed it ☐

¿Adónde fuiste de vacaciones?	Where did you go on holiday?
hace una semana / un mes / un año	a week / month / year ago
hace dos semanas / meses / años	two weeks / months / years ago
fui de vacaciones a …	I went on holiday to …
Francia / Italia / Turquía	France / Italy / Turkey
¿Con quién fuiste?	Who did you go with?
Fui …	I went …
con mi familia / insti	with my family / school
con mi mejor amigo/a	with my best friend

Módulo 1 Palabras

solo/a	*alone*	horroroso	*awful*
¿Cómo viajaste?	*How did you travel?*	un desastre	*a disaster*
Viajé …	*I travelled …*	¿Qué tiempo hizo?	*What was the weather like?*
en autocar / avión	*by coach / plane*		
en barco / coche / tren	*by boat / car / train*	Hizo buen / mal tiempo.	*It was good / bad weather.*

Had a look ☐ Nearly there ☐ Nailed it ☐

¿Qué hiciste?	**What did you do?**
primero	*first*
luego	*then*
más tarde	*later*
después	*after*
finalmente	*finally*
Lo mejor fue cuando …	*The best thing was when …*
Lo peor fue cuando …	*The worst thing was when …*

Hizo calor / frío / sol / viento. — *It was hot / cold / sunny / windy.*
Hubo niebla / tormenta. — *It was foggy / stormy.*
Llovió / Nevó. — *It rained / snowed.*

Had a look ☐ Nearly there ☐ Nailed it ☐

¿Cómo era el hotel?	**What was the hotel like?**
Me alojé / Me quedé …	*I stayed …*
Nos alojamos / Nos quedamos …	*We stayed …*
en un albergue juvenil	*in a youth hostel*
en un apartamento	*in an apartment*
en un camping	*on a campsite*
en un hotel de cinco estrellas	*in a five-star hotel*
en un parador	*in a state-run luxury hotel*
en una casa rural	*in a house in the country*
en una pensión	*in a guest house*
Fui de crucero.	*I went on a cruise.*
Estaba …	*It was …*
cerca de la playa	*near the beach*
en el centro de la ciudad	*in the city centre*
en las afueras	*on the outskirts*

Had a look ☐ Nearly there ☐ Nailed it ☐

aprendí a hacer vela	*I learned to sail*
comí muchos helados	*I ate lots of ice creams*
compré recuerdos	*I bought souvenirs*
descansé	*I rested*
fui al acuario	*I went to the aquarium*
hice turismo	*I went sightseeing*
llegué tarde al aeropuerto	*I arrived at the airport late*
perdí mi móvil	*I lost my mobile*
saqué fotos	*I took photos*
tomé el sol	*I sunbathed*
tuve un accidente en la playa	*I had an accident on the beach*
vi un partido	*I saw / watched a match*
visité el Park Güell	*I visited Park Güell*
vomité en una montaña rusa	*I was sick on a roller coaster*
Puedes …	*You can …*
descubrir el Museo Picasso	*discover the Picasso Museum*
disfrutar del Barrio Gótico	*enjoy the Gothic quarter*
pasear por las Ramblas	*walk along Las Ramblas*
subir al Monumento a Colón	*go up the Columbus Monument*
ver los barcos en el puerto	*see the boats in the port*

Era …	*It was …*
acogedor(a)	*welcoming*
antiguo/a	*old*
barato/a	*cheap*
caro/a	*expensive*
grande	*big*
lujoso/a	*luxurious*
moderno/a	*modern*
pequeño/a	*small*
ruidoso/a	*noisy*
tranquilo/a	*quiet*
Tenía / Había …	*It had / There was / were …*
No tenía ni … ni …	*It had neither … nor …*
No había ni … ni …	*There was no … nor …*
Tampoco tenía …	*Nor did it have …*
(un) aparcamiento	*a car park*
(un) bar	*a bar*
(un) gimnasio	*a gym*
(un) restaurante	*a restaurant*
(una) cafetería	*a café*
(una) lavandería	*a launderette*
(una) piscina cubierta	*an indoor pool*
mucho espacio para mi tienda	*lots of space for my tent*

Had a look ☐ Nearly there ☐ Nailed it ☐

¿Qué tal lo pasaste?	**How was it?**
Me gustó / Me encantó.	*I liked it / I loved it.*
Lo pasé bomba / fenomenal.	*I had a great time.*
Lo pasé bien / mal / fatal.	*I had a good / bad / awful time.*
Fue …	*It was …*
inolvidable / increíble	*unforgettable / incredible*
impresionante / flipante	*impressive / awesome*

M1

Módulo 1 Palabras

¿Cómo era el pueblo? — *What was the town / village like?*

Lo bueno / Lo malo …	*The good thing / The bad thing …*
del pueblo …	*about the town / village …*
de la ciudad …	*about the city …*
era que era …	*was that it was …*
demasiado / muy / bastante …	*too / very / quite …*
animado/a	*lively*
bonito/a	*pretty*
histórico/a	*historic*
pintoresco/a	*picturesque*
turístico/a	*touristic*
Tenía …	*It had …*
mucho ambiente / tráfico	*lots of atmosphere / traffic*
mucho que hacer	*lots to do*
mucha contaminación / gente	*lots of pollution / people*
muchos espacios verdes	*lots of green spaces*
muchos lugares de interés	*lots of places of interest*
muchas discotecas	*lots of discos*

Had a look ☐ Nearly there ☐ Nailed it ☐

Quisiera reservar … — *I would like to book …*

¿Hay …	*Is / Are there …*
wifi gratis …	*free wifi …*
aire acondicionado … en el hotel / las habitaciones?	*air conditioning … in the hotel / the rooms?*
¿Cuánto cuesta una habitación …?	*How much does a … room cost?*
¿A qué hora se sirve el desayuno?	*What time is breakfast served?*
¿Cuándo está abierto/a el/la …?	*When is the … open?*
¿Cuánto es el suplemento por …?	*How much is the supplement for …?*
¿Se admiten perros?	*Are dogs allowed?*
Quisiera reservar …	*I would like to book …*
una habitación individual / doble	*a single / double room*
con / sin balcón	*with / without a balcony*
con bañera / ducha	*with a bath / shower*
con cama de matrimonio	*with a double bed*
con desayuno incluido	*with breakfast included*
con media pensión	*with half board*
con pensión completa	*with full board*
con vistas al mar	*with a sea view*
¿Para cuántas noches?	*For how many nights?*
Para … noches	*For … nights*
del … al … de …	*from the … to the … of …*
¿Puede repetir, por favor?	*Can you repeat, please?*
¿Puede hablar más despacio?	*Can you speak more slowly?*

Had a look ☐ Nearly there ☐ Nailed it ☐

Quiero quejarme — *I want to complain*

Quiero hablar con el director.	*I want to speak to the manager.*
Quiero cambiar de habitación.	*I want to change rooms.*
La ducha / La habitación … está sucio/a	*The shower / The room … is dirty*
El ascensor / La luz / El aire acondicionado … no funciona	*The lift / The light / The air conditioning … doesn't work*
Hay ratas en la cama.	*There are rats in the bed.*
No hay …	*There is no …*
Necesito …	*I need …*
papel higiénico	*toilet paper*
jabón / champú	*soap / shampoo*
toallas / (un) secador	*towels / a hairdryer*
¡Socorro!	*Help!*
Es inaceptable.	*It's unacceptable.*
Lo siento / Perdone.	*I'm sorry.*
El hotel está completo.	*The hotel is full.*

Had a look ☐ Nearly there ☐ Nailed it ☐

Mis vacaciones desastrosas — *My disastrous holiday*

Por desgracia	*Unfortunately*
Por un lado … por otro lado …	*On one hand … on the other hand …*
El primer / último día	*(On) the first / last day*
Al día siguiente	*On the following day*
Tuve / Tuvimos …	*I had / We had …*
un accidente / un pinchazo	*an accident / a puncture*
un retraso / una avería	*a delay / a breakdown*
Tuve / Tuvimos que …	*I had to / We had to …*
esperar mucho tiempo	*wait a long time*
ir al hospital / a la comisaría	*go to the hospital / to the police station*
llamar a un mecánico	*call a mechanic*
Perdí / Perdimos …	*I lost / We lost …*
el equipaje / la cartera	*the luggage / the wallet*
la maleta / las llaves	*the suitcase / the keys*

Had a look ☐ Nearly there ☐ Nailed it ☐

Cuando llegamos …	*When we arrived …*
era muy tarde	*it was very late*
estaba cansado/a	*I was tired*
la recepción ya estaba cerrada	*the reception was already closed*
acampar	*to camp*
decidir	*to decide (to)*
alquilar bicicletas	*to hire bicycles*
coger el teleférico	*to catch / take the cable car*
chocar con	*to crash into*
hacer alpinismo	*to go mountain climbing*
volver	*to return*
el paisaje	*the landscape*
la autopista	*the motorway*
precioso/a	*beautiful*

Had a look ☐ Nearly there ☐ Nailed it ☐

Extra words I should know for reading and listening activities

¿Qué haces en tu tiempo libre?	What do you do in your free time?
la canoa	canoe
el centro comercial	shopping centre
chatear en la red	to communicate on the internet
descansar	to relax
echar relajo	to go wild (Mexican slang)
escalada	climbing
hacer alpinismo	to go mountain climbing
hacer deportes acuáticos	to do water sports
hacer / practicar deporte	to do sport
ir de compras	to go shopping
ir de paseo	to go for a walk
el montón de revistas	pile of magazines
la pista comando	assault course
la pista de hielo	ice rink
el refugio de animales	animal sanctuary
ser un/a líder	to be a leader
el taller creativo / de cocina / teatro / etc.	creative / cookery / theatre etc. workshop
el tiro con arco	archery
trabajar en equipo	to work in a team
usar el ordenador	to go on the computer

Had a look ☐ Nearly there ☐ Nailed it ☐

¿Qué haces cuando vas de vacaciones?	What you do when you go on holiday?
¿Adónde fuiste de vacaciones el año pasado?	Where did you go on holiday last year?
¿Dónde pasaste tus últimas vacaciones?	Where did you go on your last holiday?
broncearse	to get a tan
bucear	to swim underwater / to scuba dive
estar al aire libre	to be outside
hacer manualidades	to do handicrafts
hacer turismo	to do tourism
el helado	ice cream
inscribirse	to enroll
la insolación	sunstroke
nadar	to swim
el paisaje	landscape / scenery
el paraguas*	umbrella
pegar (el sol)	the beat down (of the sun)
el recorrido	tour
el recuerdo	souvenir
sacar fotos**	to take photos
la sombrilla	sunshade / parasol
tomar el sol	to sunbathe

Had a look ☐ Nearly there ☐ Nailed it ☐

¿Cómo viajas y dónde te alojas?	How do you travel and where do you stay?
acampar	to camp
acogedor(a)	friendly / welcoming / cosy
el albergue juvenil	youth hostel
alejado de la civilización	far from civilisation
alojarse / quedarse	to stay
alquilar un apartamento / una casa	to rent an apartment / a house
el campamento de verano	summer camp
ir al extranjero	to go abroad
ir de crucero	to go on a cruise
llegar pronto / tarde	to arrive early / late
el parador	state-run luxury hotel
Quisiera reservar una habitación.	I would like to reserve a room.
recorrer a pie	to explore on foot
el retraso	delay
tener un accidente / un pinchazo	to have an accident / a puncture
tener una avería	to break down
el trayecto	journey
viajar en coche / avión / barco / tren / autocar	to travel by car / plane / boat / train / coach

Had a look ☐ Nearly there ☐ Nailed it ☐

---

 *Work out the meaning of unfamiliar words

When trying to work out the meaning of a word look for clues. *El paraguas* combines the words *para* and *agua*, which would literally translate 'for water'. Note too that although *paraguas* ends with 's' it is a singular noun so you would say, for example, ¿Dónde está mi paraguas?

 **Pick the right verb

Don't fall into the trap of using *tomar* when you want to say 'to take a photo'. The correct verbs to use in Spanish are *sacar* or *hacer*. Example: *Siempre saco / hago muchas fotos cuando voy de vacaciones.*

Words I should know for speaking and writing activities

¿Te interesa(n) …? / Are you interested in …?

el arte dramático	drama
el dibujo	art / drawing
el español	Spanish
el inglés	English
la biología	biology
la educación física	PE
la física	physics
la geografía	geography
la historia	history
la informática	ICT
la lengua	language
la química	chemistry
la religión	RE
la tecnología	technology
los idiomas	languages
las empresariales	business studies
las matemáticas	maths
las ciencias	science
la materia / la asignatura	subject

Had a look ☐ Nearly there ☐ Nailed it ☐

me encanta(n) / me chifla(n)	I love
me interesa(n) / me fascina(n)	I'm interested in / fascinated by
me gusta(n) / no me gusta(n)	I like / I don't like
odio	I hate
prefiero	I prefer
porque es / son	because it is / they are
Mi día preferido es (el viernes).	My favourite day is (Friday).
mi horario	my timetable
¿Qué día tienes …?	What day do you have …?
Tengo inglés los martes.	I have English on Tuesdays.
¿A qué hora tienes …?	What time do you have …?
a la una / a las dos	at one o'clock / at two o'clock
y / menos cuarto	quarter past / to
y / menos cinco	five past / to
y media	half past
la educación infantil / primaria	pre-school / primary education
la educación secundaria	secondary education
el bachillerato	A levels
la formación profesional	vocational training
el instituto	secondary school

Had a look ☐ Nearly there ☐ Nailed it ☐

¿Qué tal los estudios? / How are your studies?

La física es más / menos … que …	Physics is more / less … than …
Es mejor / peor que …	It's better / worse than …
tan … como	as … as
fácil / difícil	easy / difficult
divertido/a / aburrido/a	fun / boring
útil / relevante / práctico/a	useful / relevant / practical
creativo/a / relajante	creative / relaxing
exacto/a / lógico/a	precise / logical
exigente	demanding
Mi profesor(a) (de ciencias) es …	My (science) teacher is …
paciente / impaciente	patient / impatient
tolerante / severo/a	tolerant / harsh
listo/a / tonto/a	clever / stupid
trabajador(a)	hard-working
perezoso/a	lazy
simpático/a / estricto/a	nice / strict

Had a look ☐ Nearly there ☐ Nailed it ☐

Mi profe …	My teacher …
enseña / explica bien	teaches / explains well
tiene buen sentido de humor	has a good sense of humour
tiene expectativas altas	has high expectations
crea un buen ambiente de trabajo	creates a good working atmosphere
nunca se enfada	never gets angry
me hace pensar	makes me think
nos da consejos / estrategias	gives us advice / strategies
nos pone muchos deberes	gives us lots of homework
el curso académico	academic year
las pruebas / las evaluaciones	tests / assessments
suspender / aprobar	to fail / to pass

Had a look ☐ Nearly there ☐ Nailed it ☐

¿Cómo es tu insti? / What is your school like?

En mi instituto hay …	In my school there is …
Mi instituto tiene …	My school has …
un salón de actos	a hall
un comedor	a canteen
un campo de fútbol	a football pitch
un patio	a playground
un gimnasio	a gym
una piscina	a pool
una biblioteca	a library
una pista de tenis / atletismo	a tennis court / an athletics track
unos laboratorios	some laboratories
muchas aulas	lots of classrooms
Lo bueno / malo es que …	The good / bad thing is that …
Lo mejor / peor es que …	The best / worst thing is that …
Lo que más me gusta es / son …	What I like most is / are …
Lo que menos me gusta es / son …	What I like least is / are …
no …ningún / ninguna	not a single …
ni … ni …	(n)either …(n)or

Módulo 2 Palabras

nada	nothing / anything
nadie	no one / anyone
tampoco	not either

Had a look ☐ **Nearly there** ☐ **Nailed it** ☐

Mi insti es …	My school is …
mixto / femenino / masculino	mixed / all girls / all boys
público / privado	state / private
pequeño / grande	small / large
moderno / antiguo	modern / old
En mi escuela primaria había …	In my primary school there was / were …
Mi escuela primaria tenía …	My primary school had …
más / menos …	more / fewer / less …
exámenes / deberes / alumnos	exams / homework / pupils
muebles / espacios verdes	furniture / green spaces
tiempo libre	free time
oportunidades / instalaciones	opportunities / facilities
pizarras interactivas / clases	interactive whiteboards / lessons
aulas de informática	ICT rooms
donde jugar	somewhere to play
poco espacio	little space
antes / ahora	before / now
El edificio / El colegio	The building / The school
El día escolar es / era …	The school day is / was …
(in)adecuado/a / corto/a / largo/a	(in)adequate / short / long
Las clases son / eran …	The lessons are / were …
Instituto de Educación Secundaria (IES)	secondary school

Had a look ☐ **Nearly there** ☐ **Nailed it** ☐

Las normas del insti — **School rules**

Tengo que llevar …	I have to wear …
Tenemos que llevar …	We have to wear …
(No) Llevo …	I (don't) wear …
(No) Llevamos …	We (don't) wear …
Es obligatorio llevar …	It's compulsory to wear …
un jersey (de punto)	a (knitted) sweater
un vestido	a dress
una camisa	a shirt
una camiseta	a T-shirt
una chaqueta (a rayas)	a (striped) jacket
una chaqueta de punto	a cardigan
una corbata	a tie
una falda (a cuadros)	a (checked) skirt
unos pantalones	trousers
unos calcetines	socks
unos zapatos	shoes
unos vaqueros	jeans
unas medias	tights

Had a look ☐ **Nearly there** ☐ **Nailed it** ☐

oscuro / claro	dark / light
a rayas / a cuadros	striped / checked
bonito / feo	pretty / ugly
cómodo / incómodo	comfortable / uncomfortable
anticuado / elegante / formal	old-fashioned / smart / formal
El uniforme …	Uniform …
mejora la disciplina	improves discipline
limita la individualidad	limits individuality
da una imagen positiva del insti	gives a positive image of the school
ahorra tiempo por la mañana	saves time in the morning

Had a look ☐ **Nearly there** ☐ **Nailed it** ☐

Está prohibido …	It is forbidden …
No se permite …	You are not allowed to …
No se debe …	You / One must not …
comer chicle	chew chewing gum
usar el móvil en clase	use your phone in lessons
dañar las instalaciones	damage the facilities
ser agresivo o grosero	be agressive or rude
correr en los pasillos	run in the corridors
llevar piercings	have visible piercings
Hay que …	It is necessary …
ser puntual	to be on time
respetar el turno de palabra	to wait for your turn to speak
mantener limpio el patio	to keep the playground clean
La norma más importante es …	The most important rule is …
respetar a los demás	to respect others

Had a look ☐ **Nearly there** ☐ **Nailed it** ☐

Las normas son …	The rules are …
necesarias / demasiado severas	necessary / too strict
para fomentar la buena disciplina	for promoting good discipline
para limitar la libertad de expresión	for limiting freedom of expression
para fastidiar a los alumnos	for annoying the pupils
sacar buenas / malas notas	to get good / bad grades
Estoy de acuerdo.	I agree.
¡Qué va!	No way!
¡Qué horror!	How awful!
¡Qué bien!	How great!
Un problema de mi insti es …	One problem in my school is …
el estrés de los exámenes	exam stress
el acoso escolar	bullying
la presión del grupo	peer pressure
Hay (unos) alumnos que …	There are (some) pupils who …
se burlan de otros	make fun of others

17

Módulo 2 Palabras

sufren intimidación	are victims of bullying
tienen miedo de …	are afraid of …
hacen novillos	skip lessons / skive
quieren ser parte de la pandilla	want to be part of the friendship group
son una mala influencia	are a bad influence

Had a look ☐ Nearly there ☐ Nailed it ☐

¿Cómo es tu día escolar? / What is your school day like?

normalmente	usually
Salgo de casa a las …	I leave home at …
Voy …	I go …
a pie / andando	on foot / walking
en bici / en autobús / en coche	by bike / by bus / by car
en metro / en taxi / en tren	by underground / by taxi / by train
Las clases empiezan / terminan a las …	Lessons start / finish at …
Tenemos … clases al día.	We have … lessons per day.
Cada clase dura … minutos.	Each lessons lasts … minutes.
El recreo / La hora de comer es a la(s)…	Break / Lunch is at …

Had a look ☐ Nearly there ☐ Nailed it ☐

¿Qué vas a hacer? / What are you going to do?

Voy / Vas / Vamos a …	I'm going / You're going / We're going to …
llegar / salir / estar	arrive / go out / be
ir en coche / andando	go by car / walk
llevar ropa de calle	wear casual clothes / non-uniform
ir / comer juntos	go / eat together
hacer una visita guiada	do a guided tour
ver los edificios	see the buildings
pasar todo el día en …	spend the whole day in …
asistir a clases	attend lessons
practicar el español	practise Spanish
ir de excursión	go on a trip
tener una programación variada	have a varied programme
Va a …	It's going to …
ser fácil / guay	be easy / cool

Had a look ☐ Nearly there ☐ Nailed it ☐

Las actividades extraescolares / Extra-curricular activities

Toco la trompeta …	I play / I've been playing the trumpet …
Canto en el coro …	I sing / I've been singing in the choir …
Voy al club de …	I go / I've been going to the … club
Soy miembro del club de …	I am / I've been a member of the … club
ajedrez / judo / teatro / periodismo	chess / judo / drama / reporters
lectores / Ecoescuela / fotografía	reading / eco-schools / photography
desde hace … años / meses	for … years / months

Had a look ☐ Nearly there ☐ Nailed it ☐

Para mí …	For me …
Pienso que / Creo que …	I think that …
las actividades extraescolares son …	extra-curricular activities are …
muy divertidas	a lot of fun
algo diferente / un éxito	something different / an achievement
te ayudan a …	they help you to …
olvidar las presiones del colegio	forget the pressures of school
desarrollar tus talentos	develop your talents
hacer nuevos amigos	make new friends
te dan …	they give you …
una sensación de logro	a sense of achievement
más confianza	more confidence
la oportunidad de ser creativo/a	the opportunity to be creative
la oportunidad de expresarte	the opportunity to express yourself

Had a look ☐ Nearly there ☐ Nailed it ☐

El año / trimestre / verano pasado …	Last year / term / summer …
participé en un evento especial	I took part in a special event
un concierto / un concurso / un torneo	a concert / a competition / a tournament
gané un trofeo	I won a trophy
toqué un solo	I played a solo
conseguimos la clasificación	we achieved the award / designation
como …	as …
tuvimos una charla	we had a talk / presentation
ganamos una competición nacional	we won a national competition
dimos un concierto	we gave a concert
¡Fue un éxito!	It was a success!
Este trimestre / El próximo trimestre …	This term / Next term …
voy a	I'm going to …
aprender a …	learn to …
continuar con …	continue with …
dejarlo	stop doing it
apuntarme al club de …	sign up for the … club
vamos a …	we are going to …
montar una obra de teatro	put on a play
conseguir	achieve

Had a look ☐ Nearly there ☐ Nailed it ☐

Módulo 2 Palabras

Extra words I should know for reading and listening activities

Lo que hacemos en el insti	What we do at school
apoyar	to support / to back / to help
castigar	to punish
conseguir	to get / to achieve
contestar	to answer
dar la bienvenida*	to welcome
dejar en paz	to leave alone / in peace
enseñar	to teach
entregar	to hand in
esforzarse	to make an effort
estudiar	to study
exigir	to demand
ganar	to win
lograr	to achieve
mejorar	to improve
memorizar	to memorise
pedir prestado	to borrow
refugiarse	to take refuge
restringir	to restrict
saber	to know
tocar la trompeta / el saxofón etc.**	to play the trumpet / saxophone etc.

Had a look ☐ **Nearly there** ☐ **Nailed it** ☐

Lo que hay en el insti	What there is at school
la academia	academy / school post-16 (for certain careers)
el apoyo	help / support / backing
la carpeta	folder / file
el castigo	punishment
clases intensivas de refuerzo escolar	intensive revision classes
clases particulares	private lessons
el/la compañero/a	fellow student
el despacho	office
edificios modernos / antiguos / recién renovados	modern / old / recently renovated buildings
la enseñanza	teaching / education
la ESO (Educación Secundaria Obligatoria)	secondary education from 12 to 16 years old
el intercambio	exchange
el internado	boarding school
la lectura	reading
la libertad de expresión	freedom of expression
el patio cubierto	covered playground
el polideportivo	sports hall
el salón de actos	auditorium / assembly hall

Had a look ☐ **Nearly there** ☐ **Nailed it** ☐

Expresiones y descripciones	Expressions and descriptions
¡No es justo!	It isn't fair!
¿Qué opinas de …?	What do you think about …?
apropiado	appropriate
bien equipado	well-equipped
el uniforme limita la individualidad	uniform limits your individuality
es la asignatura más exigente	it's the most demanding subject
los amigos cuentan más	friends are more important
me fastidia …	… annoys me
me hace pensar	he/she/it makes me think
me inspiró mucho	it inspired me a lot
mi profe me deja trabajar a mi manera	my teacher lets me work in my own way
mi profesor me cae bien	I like my teacher
nos ofrece más oportunidades	it gives us more opportunities
repetir los exámenes	resit exams
superestresado/a	highly stressed

Had a look ☐ **Nearly there** ☐ **Nailed it** ☐

⭐ ***Break unfamiliar words to work out their meaning**

If you know the meanings of component parts of unfamiliar words and phrases you can often work out what they mean. So for example the component parts of *dar la bienvenida* are:
dar to give
bien well
venida from *venir* to come

⭐ ****Learn and use the right verbs**

To play an instrument in Spanish is *tocar un instrumento*. Don't fall into the trap of using the verb *jugar*.
Note too that the spelling of the 'I' form in the preterite changes.
Example: *Toqué el piano ayer.*

Módulo 3 Palabras

Words I should know for speaking and writing activities

¿Qué aplicaciones usas?	What apps do you use?
Uso ... para ...	I use ... (in order) to ...
ver mis series favoritas	watch my favourite series
organizar las salidas con mis amigos	organise to go out with my friends
controlar mi actividad física / las calorías	monitor my physical activity / my calorie intake
contactar con mi familia	get in touch with my family
chatear con mis amigos	chat with my friends
La tengo desde hace ... meses	I've had it for ... months
Es una aplicación buena para ...	It's a good app for ...
buscar y descargar música	looking for and downloading music
pasar el tiempo / el rato	passing the time
sacar / editar / personalizar fotos	taking / editing / personalising photos
compartir / subir fotos	sharing / uploading photos
estar en contacto	keeping in touch
conocer a nueva gente	meeting new people
subir y ver vídeos	uploading and watching videos
chatear y mandar mensajes	chatting and sending messages

Had a look ☐ **Nearly there** ☐ **Nailed it** ☐

Es / No es ...	It is / It isn't ...
una red social	a social network
amplio/a	extensive
cómodo/a	convenient
divertido/a	fun
necesario/a	necessary
peligroso/a	dangerous
práctico/a	practical
rápido/a	quick
fácil de usar	easy to use
popular	popular
útil	useful
gratis	free
un canal de comunicación	a channel / means of communication
una pérdida de tiempo	a waste of time
Soy / Es adicto/a a ...	I am / He/She is addicted to ...
Estoy / Está enganchado/a a ...	I am / He/She is hooked on ...
Lo único malo es que ...	The only bad thing is that ...
te engancha	it gets you hooked

Had a look ☐ **Nearly there** ☐ **Nailed it** ☐

¿Qué estás haciendo?	What are you doing?
Estoy ...	I am ...
actualizando mi página de Facebook	updating my Facebook page
editando mis fotos	editing my photos
Estás / Está / Están ...	You are / He/She is / They are ...
escuchando música	listening to music
esperando a (David)	waiting for (David)
descansando	relaxing
pensando en salir	thinking about going out
preparando algo para merendar	preparing something for tea
repasando para un examen	revising for an exam
tomando el sol	sunbathing
haciendo footing	jogging
haciendo el vago	lazing about
leyendo	reading
viendo una peli	watching a film
escribiendo	writing

Had a look ☐ **Nearly there** ☐ **Nailed it** ☐

¿Quieres salir conmigo?	Do you want to go out with me?
No puedo porque ...	I can't because ...
está lloviendo	it's raining
tengo que ...	I have to ...
salir	go out
visitar a (mi abuela)	visit (my grandmother)
cuidar a (mi hermano)	look after (my brother)
hacer los deberes	do homework
quiero ...	I want ...
subir mis fotos a ...	to upload my photos to ...
quedarme en casa	to stay at home
¡Qué rollo!	What a pain!
¿A qué hora quedamos?	What time shall we meet?
¿Dónde quedamos?	Where shall we meet?
en la Plaza Mayor	in the main square
debajo de	underneath
detrás de	behind
delante de	in front of
enfrente de	opposite
al lado de	next to

Had a look ☐ **Nearly there** ☐ **Nailed it** ☐

¿Qué te gusta leer?	What do you like reading?
los blogs	blogs
los tebeos / los cómics	comics
los periódicos	newspapers
las revistas	magazines
las poesías	poems
las novelas de ciencia ficción	science fiction novels

Módulo 3 Palabras

las novelas de amor — *romantic novels*
las historias de vampiros — *vampire stories*
las biografías — *biographies*

Had a look ☐ Nearly there ☐ Nailed it ☐

¿Con qué frecuencia lees? — *How often do you read?*
cada día / todos los días — *every day*
a menudo — *often*
generalmente — *generally*
de vez en cuando — *from time to time*
una vez a la semana — *once a week*
dos veces al mes — *twice a month*
una vez al año — *once a year*
nunca — *never*

Had a look ☐ Nearly there ☐ Nailed it ☐

¿Qué es mejor, leer en papel o en la red? — *What's better, reading paper books or online?*
Leer en formato digital ... — *Reading in digital format ...*
protege el planeta — *protects the planet*
no malgasta papel — *doesn't waste paper*
cansa la vista — *tires your eyes*
depende de la energía eléctrica — *relies on electricity*
te permite llevar contigo miles de libros — *allows you to take thousands of books with you*
cuesta mucho menos — *costs a lot less*
fastidia porque no hay numeración de páginas — *is annoying because there is no page numbering*
Los libros electrónicos / Los e-books ... — *Electronic books / E-books ...*
son fáciles de transportar — *are easy to transport*
son más ecológicos / baratos — *are more environmentally friendly / cheaper*
no ocupan espacio — *don't take up space*

Had a look ☐ Nearly there ☐ Nailed it ☐

Una desventaja es ... — *One disadvantage is ...*
el uso de batería — *the battery use*
Me gusta / Prefiero ... — *I like / I prefer ...*
tocar las páginas — *to touch the pages*
pasar las páginas a mano — *to turn the pages by hand*
escribir anotaciones — *to write notes*
leer horas y horas — *to read for hours and hours*
un ratón de biblioteca — *a bookworm*
un fan del manga — *a manga fan*
un libro tradicional — *a traditional book*
un libro de verdad — *a real book*

Had a look ☐ Nearly there ☐ Nailed it ☐

La familia — *Family*
el padre / la madre — *father / mother*
el padrastro / la madrastra — *step-father / step-mother*
el hermano / la hermana — *brother / sister*
el hermanastro / la hermanastra — *step-brother / step-sister*
el abuelo / la abuela — *grandfather / grandmother*
el bisabuelo / la bisabuela — *great grandfather / great grandmother*
el tío / la tía — *uncle / aunt*
el primo / la prima — *male cousin / female cousin*
el sobrino / la sobrina — *nephew / niece*
el marido / la mujer — *husband / wife*
el hijo / la hija — *son / daughter*
el nieto / la nieta — *grandson / granddaughter*
mayor / menor — *older / younger*

Had a look ☐ Nearly there ☐ Nailed it ☐

¿Cómo es? — *What is he/she like?*
Tiene los ojos ... — *He/She has ... eyes*
azules / verdes / marrones / grises — *blue / green / brown / grey*
grandes / pequeños / brillantes — *big / small / bright*
Tiene el pelo ... — *He/She has ... hair*
moreno / rubio / castaño / rojo — *dark brown / blond / mid-brown / red*
corto / largo — *short / long*
rizado / liso / ondulado — *curly / straight / wavy*
fino / de punta — *fine / spiky*

Had a look ☐ Nearly there ☐ Nailed it ☐

Tiene ... — *He/She has ...*
la piel blanca / morena — *fair / dark skin*
la cara redonda / alargada — *a round / oval face*
los dientes prominentes — *big teeth*
pecas — *freckles*
Lleva ... — *He/She wears / has ...*
gafas — *glasses*
barba — *a beard*
bigote — *a moustache*
Es ... — *He/She is ...*
alto/a / bajo/a — *tall / short*
delgado/a / gordito/a / gordo/a — *slim / chubby / fat*
calvo/a — *bald*
moreno/a — *dark-haired*
rubio/a — *fair-haired*
castaño/a — *brown-haired*
pelirrojo/a — *a redhead*
español / española — *Spanish*
inglés / inglesa — *English*
peruano / peruana — *Peruvian*

M 3

Módulo 3 Palabras

Mide 1, 60.	He/She is 1m60 tall.
No es ni alto ni bajo.	He/She is neither tall nor short.
(No) Nos parecemos físicamente.	We (don't) look like each other.

Had a look ☐ **Nearly there** ☐ **Nailed it** ☐

¿Cómo es de carácter? / What is he/she like as a person?

Como persona, es …	As a person, he/she is …
optimista / pesimista	optimistic / pessimistic
simpático/a / antipático/a	nice / nasty
trabajador(a) / perezoso/a	hard-working / lazy
generoso/a / tacaño/a	generous / mean
hablador(a) / callado/a	chatty / quiet
divertido/a / gracioso/a / serio/a	fun / funny / serious
fiel / infiel	loyal / disloyal
feliz / triste	happy / sad
ordenado/a / caótico/a	tidy / chaotic
enérgico/a / animado/a / tranquilo/a	energetic / lively / calm
pensativo/a	thoughtful
comprensivo/a	understanding
honesto/a	honest
alegre	cheerful
molesto/a	annoying
ambicioso/a	ambitious
egoísta	selfish
Está feliz / triste.	He/She is happy / sad.

Had a look ☐ **Nearly there** ☐ **Nailed it** ☐

¿Te llevas bien con tu familia? / Do you get on well with your family?

(No) Me llevo bien con … porque …	I (don't) get on well with … because …
me apoya	he/she supports me
me acepta como soy	he/she accepts me as I am
nunca me critica	he/she never criticises me
tenemos mucho en común	we have a lot in common
Me divierto con …	I have a good time with …
Me peleo con …	I argue with …
Nos llevamos superbién.	We get on really well.
Nos llevamos como el perro y el gato.	We fight like cat and dog.
Nos divertimos siempre.	We always have a good time.

Had a look ☐ **Nearly there** ☐ **Nailed it** ☐

¿Cómo es un buen amigo / una buena amiga? / What is a good friend like?

Un buen amigo es alguien que …	A good friend is someone who …
te apoya	supports you
te escucha	listens to you
te conoce bien	knows you well
te acepta como eres	accepts you as you are
te quiere mucho	likes / loves you a lot
te da consejos	gives you advice
te hace reír	makes you laugh
no te critica	doesn't criticise you
nunca te juzga	never judges you
Conocí a mi mejor amigo/a …	I met my best friend …
Nos conocimos	We met / got to know each other
Nos hicimos amigos	We became friends
Nos hicimos novios	We started going out
convivimos	we lived together
nos casamos	we got married
Es el amor de mi vida.	He/She is the love of my life.
Tenemos … en común.	We have … in common.
nos gustan (las mismas cosas)	we like (the same things)
nos encantan (las películas)	we love (films)

Had a look ☐ **Nearly there** ☐ **Nailed it** ☐

Extra words I should know for reading and listening activities

Describiendo a una persona / *Describing someone*

atrevido/a	cheeky / insolent / bold / daring
celoso/a	jealous
cómico/a	comical
cuidadoso/a	careful
dinámico/a	dynamic
educado/a*	polite
Es tan tranquilo/a como el agua de un pozo.**	(lit.) He/She is as calm as water in a well.
explosivo/a	explosive
histérico/a	hysterical
idealista	idealistic
modesto/a	modest
no se impacienta nunca con nadie	he/she never loses his/her patience with anyone
No se pelea nunca.	He/She doesn't ever argue.
paciente	patient
romántico/a	romantic
seguro/a de sí mismo	self-assured
sincero/a	sincere
sus ojos son tan pequeños como dos botones / grandes / redondos	his/her eyes are as small as two big / round buttons
tiene el pelo negro como el carbón	her hair is as black as coal
tímido/a	shy
travieso/a	naughty

Had a look ☐ Nearly there ☐ Nailed it ☐

Relacionándose con la gente / *Relating to people*

aconsejar	to advise
acordar	to agree on
aguantar	to bear / to put up with
agradecer	to thank / to be grateful for
asentir	to nod
celebrar	to celebrate
chatear	to chat / to talk
confiar	to trust
corroborar	to agree / to corroborate
despedir(se)	to say goodbye
disculpar(se)	to apologise
hacer multitarea	to multitask
llorar	to cry
ocuparse de	to look after
parecerse a	to look like
recargar	to recharge
relacionarse con	to make contact with / to get on with (people)
(no) tener mucho en común	(not) to have much in common
tratar (de / con)	to treat each other / to have dealings with

Had a look ☐ Nearly there ☐ Nailed it ☐

Relaciones de pareja / *Partnerships*

el anillo	ring
la boda	wedding
comprometerse	to get engaged
el compromiso	engagement / commitment
el esposo	husband / spouse
el estado civil	marital status
el matrimonio	marriage
la pareja	couple / partner
separarse	to separate / to split up
el/la viudo/a	widower/widow

Had a look ☐ Nearly there ☐ Nailed it ☐

---

*Watch out for false friends

When you describe someone as being *educado* in Spanish, for example *Mi padre es muy educado*, you are not talking about your father's education, you are saying that your father is very 'polite'. If you wanted to say that someone is 'rude' or 'impolite' you would use *maleducado*.

**Don't always try to translate word for word

The literal translation of *Es tan tranquilo como el agua de un pozo* doesn't sound very good in English although it is useful to note that *pozo* means 'well'. When this happens, try to find an equivalent phrase. You could for example translate the Spanish simile with another simile in English, for example 'She is as cool as a cucumber.'

Words I should know for speaking and writing activities

La paga / Pocket money
Mis padres me dan … / My parents give me …
Mi madre / padre me da … / My mum / dad gives me …
…euros a la semana / al mes / …euros a week / a month
Gasto mi paga en … / I spend my pocket money on …
También compro … / I also buy …
saldo para el móvil / credit for my phone
ropa / joyas / maquillaje / clothes / jewellery / make-up
zapatillas de marca / designer trainers
videojuegos / revistas / computer games / magazines

Had a look ☐ Nearly there ☐ Nailed it ☐

Mis ratos libres / My free time
las actividades de ocio / leisure activities
Tengo muchos pasatiempos. / I have lots of hobbies.
A la hora de comer … / At lunchtime …
Cuando tengo tiempo … / When I have time …
Después del insti … / After school …
Los fines de semana … / At weekends …
Mientras desayuno / como … / Whilst I have breakfast / lunch …
juego al billar / futbolín / I play billiards / table football
monto en bici / monopatín / I ride my bike / I skateboard
quedo con mis amigos / I meet up with friends
voy de compras / I go shopping
mi pasión es la música / la lectura / my passion is music / reading

Had a look ☐ Nearly there ☐ Nailed it ☐

Suelo … / I tend to / I usually …
descansar / rest
escuchar música / la radio / listen to music / the radio
hacer deporte / do sport
ir al cine / go to the cinema
leer libros / revistas / periódicos / read books / magazines / newspapers
salir con amigos / go out with friends
usar el ordenador / use the computer
ver la tele / watch TV
Es divertido / relajante / sano / It's fun / relaxing / healthy
Soy creativo/a / perezoso/a / sociable / I'm creative / lazy / sociable
Soy adicto/a a … / I'm addicted to …
me ayuda a relajarme / it helps me to relax
me ayuda a olvidarme de todo / it helps me to forget everything

me hace reír / it makes me laugh
necesito comunicarme / relacionarme con otra gente / I need to have contact with other people

Had a look ☐ Nearly there ☐ Nailed it ☐

La música / Music
Me gusta el soul / el rap / el dance / el hip-hop / el pop / el rock / el jazz / la música clásica / electrónica / I like soul / rap / dance / hip-hop / pop / rock / jazz / classical / electronic music
asistir a un concierto / to attend a concert
cantar (una canción) / to sing (a song)
tocar el teclado / el piano / la batería / la flauta / la guitarra / la trompeta / to play the keyboard / the piano / the drums / the flute / the guitar / the trumpet
mi cantante preferido/a es … / my favourite singer is …
un espectáculo / a show
una gira (mundial) / a (world) tour

Had a look ☐ Nearly there ☐ Nailed it ☐

El deporte / Sport
Soy / Era … / I am / I used to be …
(bastante / muy) deportista / (quite / very) sporty
miembro de un club / un equipo / a member of a club / a team
aficionado/a / hincha de … / a fan of …
un(a) fanático/a de … / a … fanatic
juego al … / I play …
jugué … / I played …
jugaba al … / I used to play …
bádminton / baloncesto / badminton / basketball
béisbol / balonmano / baseball / handball
críquet / fútbol / cricket / football
hockey / ping-pong / hockey / table tennis
rugby / tenis / voleibol / rugby / tennis / volleyball

Had a look ☐ Nearly there ☐ Nailed it ☐

hago … / I do …
hice … / I did …
hacía … / I used to do …
baile / boxeo / ciclismo / dancing / boxing / cycling
deportes acuáticos / water sports
equitación / escalada / horseriding / climbing
gimnasia / judo / gymnastics / judo
kárate / natación / karate / swimming
patinaje sobre hielo / ice skating
piragüismo / remo / canoeing / rowing
submarinismo / diving
tiro con arco / archery
voy … / I go …

Módulo 4 Palabras

Spanish	English
fui …	I went …
iba …	I used to go …
a clases de …	to … classes
de pesca	fishing

Had a look ☐ **Nearly there** ☐ **Nailed it** ☐

Spanish	English
ya no (juego) …	(I) no longer (play) …
todavía (hago) …	(I) still (do) …
batir un récord	to break a record
correr	to run
entrenar	to train
jugar un partido contra …	to play a match against …
marcar un gol	to score a goal
montar a caballo	to go horseriding
participar en un torneo	to participate in a tournament
patinar	to skate
Mi jugador(a) preferido/a es …	My favourite player is …
Su punto culminante fue cuando …	The highlight (of his/her career) was when …
el campeón / la campeona	the champion
la temporada	the season

Had a look ☐ **Nearly there** ☐ **Nailed it** ☐

La tele / TV

(No) Soy teleadicto/a.	I'm (not) a TV addict.
Mi programa favorito es …	My favourite programme is …
un concurso	a game / quiz show
un programa de deportes	a sports programme
un reality	a reality TV show
un documental	a documentary
un culebrón / una telenovela	a soap
una comedia	a comedy
una serie policíaca	a crime series
el telediario / las noticias	the news
Me gustan las comedias.	I like comedies.
Es / Son …	It is / They are …
aburrido/a/os/as	boring
adictivo/a/os/as	addictive
divertido/a/os/as	fun
entretenido/a/os/as	entertaining
tonto/a/os/as	silly
informativo/a/os/as	informative
malo/a/os/as	bad
emocionante(s)	exciting
interesante(s)	interesting

Had a look ☐ **Nearly there** ☐ **Nailed it** ☐

Las películas / Films

Spanish	English
un misterio	a mystery
una película de amor	a love film
una película de terror	a horror film
una película de acción	an action film
una película de aventuras	an adventure film
una película de animación	an animated film
una película de ciencia ficción	a sci-fi film
una película de fantasía	a fantasy film
una película extranjera	a foreign film

Had a look ☐ **Nearly there** ☐ **Nailed it** ☐

Nacionalidades / Nationalities

americano/a	American
argentino/a	Argentinian
británico/a	British
chino/a	Chinese
griego/a	Greek
italiano/a	Italian
mexicano/a	Mexican
sueco/a	Swedish
alemán/alemana	German
danés/danesa	Danish
español(a)	Spanish
francés/francesa	French
holandés/holandesa	Dutch
inglés/inglesa	English
irlandés/irlandesa	Irish
japonés/japonesa	Japanese

Had a look ☐ **Nearly there** ☐ **Nailed it** ☐

Temas del momento / Trending topics

he compartido …	I have shared …
he comprado …	I have bought …
he jugado …	I have played …
he leído …	I have read …
he oído …	I have heard …
he roto …	I have broken …
he subido …	I have uploaded …
¿Has probado …?	Have you tried …?
mi hermano ha descargado …	my brother has downloaded …
se ha estrenado …	… has been released.
la nueva canción	the new song
el último libro	the latest book

Had a look ☐ **Nearly there** ☐ **Nailed it** ☐

Spanish	English
Ya lo/la/los/las he visto.	I have already seen it/them.
No lo/la/los/las he visto todavía.	I haven't seen it/them yet.
acabo de ver / jugar a …	I have just seen / played …
cuenta la historia de …	it tells the story of …
trata de …	it's about …
combina el misterio con la acción	it combines mystery with action
el argumento es fuerte / débil	the plot is strong / weak
la banda sonora es buena / mala	the soundtrack is good / bad
los actores …	the actors …

Módulo 4 Palabras

los efectos especiales ...	the special effects ...
los gráficos ...	the graphics ...
los personajes ...	the characters ...
las animaciones ...	the animations ...
las canciones ...	the songs ...
son guapos/as / guay	are good looking / cool
son estupendos/as / impresionantes	are great / impressive
son originales / repetitivos/as	are original / repetitive

Had a look ☐ Nearly there ☐ Nailed it ☐

Ir al cine, al teatro, etc. / Going to the cinema, theatre, etc.

¿Qué vamos a hacer ... esta tarde?	What are we going to do ... this afternoon / evening?
esta noche?	tonight?
mañana / el viernes?	tomorrow / on Friday?
¿Tienes ganas de ir ...	Do you fancy going ...
a un concierto / un festival?	to a concert / a festival?
a un espectáculo de baile?	to a dance show?
al cine / al teatro / al circo?	to the cinema / theatre / circus?
¿Qué ponen?	What's on?
Es una película / obra de ...	It's a ... film / play
¿A qué hora empieza / termina?	What time does it start / finish?
Empieza / Termina a las ...	It starts / finishes at ...
Dos entradas para ... / por favor para la sesión de las ...	Two tickets for ... / please for the ... showing / performance
No quedan entradas.	There are no tickets left.
¿Hay un descuento para estudiantes?	Is there a discount for students?
Aquí tiene mi carné de estudiante.	Here is my student card.

Had a look ☐ Nearly there ☐ Nailed it ☐

¿En el cine o en casa? / At the cinema or at home?

(No) Me gusta ir al cine porque ...	I (don't) like going to the cinema because ...
Prefiero ver las pelis en casa porque ...	I prefer watching films at home because ...
el ambiente es mejor	the atmosphere is better
hay demasiadas personas	there are too many people
la imagen es mejor en la gran pantalla	the picture is better on the big screen
las entradas son muy caras	the tickets are very expensive
las palomitas están ricas	the popcorn is tasty
los asientos no son cómodos	the seats aren't comfortable
los otros espectadores me molestan	the other spectators annoy me
ponen tráilers para las nuevas pelis	they show trailers for the new films
si vas al baño te pierdes una parte	if you go to the toilet you miss part of it
tienes que hacer cola	you have to queue
una corrida de toros en directo	a bull fight live

Had a look ☐ Nearly there ☐ Nailed it ☐

Los modelos a seguir / Role models

Admiro a ...	I admire ...
Mi inspiración / ídolo es ...	My inspiration / idol is ...
...es un buen / mal modelo a seguir	... is a good / bad role model
Un buen modelo a seguir es alguien que ...	A good role model is someone who ...
apoya a organizaciones benéficas	supports charities
recauda fondos para ...	raises money for ...
tiene mucho talento / éxito	is very talented / successful
trabaja en defensa de los animales	works in defence of animals
usa su fama para ayudar a los demás	uses his / her fame to help others
se emborrachan	they get drunk
se comportan mal	they behave badly
se meten en problemas con la policía	they get into problems with the police

Had a look ☐ Nearly there ☐ Nailed it ☐

es amable / cariñoso/a / fuerte	he/she is nice / affectionate / strong
lucha por / contra ...	he/she fights for / against ...
la pobreza / la homofobia	poverty / homophobia
los derechos de la mujer	women's rights
los derechos de los refugiados	the rights of refugees
los niños desfavorecidos	underprivileged children
la justicia social	social justice
a pesar de sus problemas ...	despite his/her problems ...
ha batido varios récords	he/she has broken several records
ha creado ...	he/she has created ...
ha ganado ... medallas / premios	he/she has won ... medals / awards
ha sufrido varias enfermedades	he/she has suffered several illnesses
ha superado sus problemas	he/she has overcome his/ her problems
ha tenido mucho éxito como ...	he/she has had lots of success as ...
siempre sonríe	he/she always smiles
solo piensa en los demás	he/she only thinks of other people

Had a look ☐ Nearly there ☐ Nailed it ☐

Módulo 4 Palabras

Extra words I should know for reading and listening activities

Verbos útiles	Useful verbs
acoger a (niños)	to take in (children)
aplaudir	to clap
combatir la injusticia	to fight injustice
disfrutar	to enjoy
entrar en el escenario	to come on stage
escaparse de casa	to run away from home
estrenarse	to be released
ganar* (dinero)	to earn (money)
gritar	to shout
jugar al pádel**	to play padel tennis (kind of racquet game that started in Mexico)
poner en escena	to stage
recibir	to get / to receive
recorrer	to cover (distance)
salir al mercado	to come out on the market
sobrevivir	to survive
sonreír	to smile
superar	to overcome
tener éxito	to be successful
vivir en las calles	to live on the streets

Had a look ☐   Nearly there ☐   Nailed it ☐

Expresiones y adjetivos	Expressions and adjectives
¡Es un crack!	He's a real champion.
de todos los géneros	of all kinds
decepcionante	disappointing
disponible	available
El deporte es mi vida.	Sport means everything to me.
en versión original	undubbed / original version
enganchado/a	hooked
hilarante	hilarious
Las canciones eran pegadizas.	The songs were catchy.
Me ayuda a desconectar / olvidarme de todo.	It helps me to disconnect / forget about everything else.
¡Qué ilusión!	How exciting!
¡Qué timo!	What a rip-off!
Soy un/a adicto/a a la adrenalina.	I get a rush from adrenaline.
Tiene una voz hermosa.	He/She has a lovely voice / sings beautifully.
valiente	brave

Had a look ☐   Nearly there ☐   Nailed it ☐

Nombres útiles	Useful nouns
el argumento	plot
la carrera profesional	professional career
el comportamiento	behaviour
el/la delantero/a	forward (sport)
el ejemplar	copy (of a book)
un/a embajador(a) de buena voluntad	a goodwill ambassador
el equipo de fútbol femenino	women's football team
el estilo libre	crawl / free style (swimming)
el estilo mariposa	butterfly stroke (swimming)
la estrella	star / champion (in sport)
el estreno	release (of a film / record etc.)
el/la ganador(a)	winner
el/la goleador(a)	scorer
el héroe anónimo	unsung hero
el/la jugador(a)	player
la lesión	injury
una noche inolvidable	a night to remember
la resistencia física y mental	physical and mental stamina
la taquilla	ticket office
el título mundial	world record

Had a look ☐   Nearly there ☐   Nailed it ☐

⭐ ***Use context to work out translations of words with more than one meaning**

The verb *ganar* can mean 'to earn', 'to win' or 'to gain'. When you are reading or listening, work out the correct meaning from the context. Look at the sentences below and work out the different meanings:

Para **ganar** dinero, normalmente ayudo a mis padres con algunas tareas en casa.

En julio cantamos en un concurso nacional y lo **ganamos**.

Ganará mucha experiencia trabajando como voluntario.

 ****Learn irregular verb forms and spelling changes**

Remember that *jugar* is one of the verbs in which the spelling changes for the 'I' form of the preterite, for example, *Juego al fútbol todos los días.* → *Jugué al fútbol ayer.*

Módulo 5 Palabras

Words I should know for speaking and writing activities

En mi ciudad
Hay ... / Mi ciudad tiene ...
un ayuntamiento
un bar / muchos bares
un castillo (en ruinas)
un cine
un mercado
un museo / unos museos
un parque
un polideportivo
un puerto
muchos restaurantes
un teatro
una biblioteca
una bolera
una iglesia
una piscina
una playa / unas playas
una Plaza Mayor
una pista de hielo
una oficina de Correos
una tienda / muchas tiendas
muchos lugares de interés
algo / mucho que hacer
no hay nada que hacer

In my town
There is/are ... / My town has ...
a town hall
a bar / lots of bars
a (ruined) castle
a cinema
a market
a museum / a few museums
a park
a sports centre
a port
lots of restaurants
a theatre
a library
a bowling alley
a church
a swimming pool
a beach / some beaches
a town square
an ice rink
a post office
a shop / lots of shops

lots of sights

something / a lot to do
there is nothing to do

Had a look ☐ Nearly there ☐ Nailed it ☐

Vivo en un pueblo ...
histórico / moderno
tranquilo / ruidoso
turístico / industrial
bonito / feo
Está situado/a en ... del país.
el norte / el sur
el este / el oeste

I live in a ... village
historic / modern
quiet / noisy
touristy / industrial
pretty / ugly
It is situated in ... of the country.
the north / the south /
the east / the west

Had a look ☐ Nearly there ☐ Nailed it ☐

¿Por dónde se va al / a la ...?
¿Dónde está el / la ...?
¿El / La ... está cerca / lejos de aquí?
sigue todo recto
gira a la derecha / izquierda
toma la primera / segunda / tercera calle a la derecha / a la izquierda
pasa el puente / los semáforos
cruza la plaza / la calle

How do you get to the ...?
Where is the ...?
Is the ... nearby / far away from here?
go straight on
turn right / left

take the first / second / third road on the right / left

go over the bridge / the traffic lights
cross the square / the street

coge el autobús número 37
está ...
en la esquina / al final de la calle
al lado del museo
enfrente de ...

take the number 37 bus

it is ...
on the corner / at the end of the street
next to the museum
opposite ...

Had a look ☐ Nearly there ☐ Nailed it ☐

¿Cómo es tu zona?
está situado/a en un valle
entre el desierto y la sierra
al lado del río / mar Mediterráneo
Está ...
rodeado/a de volcanes / sierra
lleno/a de bosques / selvas
a ... metros sobre el nivel del mar
Tiene ...
unos impresionantes paisajes naturales
varias influencias culturales
el bullicio de la ciudad
El clima es ...
soleado / caluroso / seco / templado / frío
llueve (muy) poco / a menudo
en primavera / verano / otoño / invierno
hay mucha marcha

What is your area like?
it is situated in a valley
between the desert and the mountains
by the river / Mediterranean sea
It is ...
surrounded by volcanoes / mountains
full of woods / forests

at ... metres above the sea level
It has ...
some amazing natural landscapes
various cultural influences
the hustle and bustle of a city
The climate is ...
sunny / hot / dry / mild / cold
it rains (very) little / often

in spring / summer / autumn / winter
there is lots going on

Had a look ☐ Nearly there ☐ Nailed it ☐

Es ...
mi ciudad natal / mi lugar favorito
acogedor/a / atractivo/a
famoso/a / conocido/a por
una región muy húmeda
una zona muy montañosa / pintoresca
tan fácil desplazarse
Se puede ...
estar mucho tiempo al aire libre
subir a la torre
hacer un recorrido en autobús
disfrutar de las vistas / del ambiente

It is ...
my home town / my favourite place
welcoming / attractive
famous for / well-known for
a very humid region
a mountainous / picturesque area
so easy to get around
You / One can ...
spend lots of time in the open air
go up the tower
do a bus tour

enjoy the views / the atmosphere

Módulo 5 Palabras

viajar en el AVE	travel on the AVE high-speed train	Estoy (muy) a gusto.	I am feeling (very much) at home.
pasear por los lagos artificiales	go boating on the artificial lakes	¡Buena idea!	Good idea!
		De acuerdo.	OK.
apreciar la arquitectura variada	appreciate the variety of architecture	¡Qué pena! / ¡Qué mal (rollo)!	What a shame! / What a nightmare!
aprovechar el buen tiempo	make the most of the good weather	¡Qué triste!	How sad!
Se pueden …	You / One can …	**Had a look** ☐ **Nearly there** ☐ **Nailed it** ☐	
probar platos típicos	try local dishes	¿Qué tiempo hará?	**What will be weather be like?**
practicar deportes acuáticos	do water sports	Hará sol / viento.	It will be sunny / windy.
ver edificios de estilos muy diferentes	see buildings with very different styles	Habrá …	There will be …
		nubes / claros / chubascos	clouds / clear spells / showers
alquilar bolas de agua	hire water balls	una ola de calor	a heat wave
practicar senderismo y ciclismo	go hiking / trekking and cycling	truenos y relámpagos	thunder and lightning
		temperaturas más altas / bajas	higher / lower temperatures
Had a look ☐ **Nearly there** ☐ **Nailed it** ☐		granizo / brisas fuertes	hail / strong winds
En la oficina de turismo	**At the tourist office**	periodos soleados	sunny spells
		lloverá (bastante)	it will rain (quite a bit)
¿Me puede dar …?	Can you give me …?	Las temperaturas subirán / bajarán.	The temperatures will rise / fall.
un plano de la ciudad	a map of the town / city		
más información sobre …	more information about …	El tiempo …	The weather …
		será variable	will be variable
¿Cuánto cuesta una entrada?	How much is a ticket?	se despejará	will clear up
		cambiará	will change
para adultos / niños	for adults / children	no nos importará	will not matter to us
¿Dónde se pueden sacar las entradas?	Where can you get tickets?	**Had a look** ☐ **Nearly there** ☐ **Nailed it** ☐	
¿A qué hora …?	What time …?	**Las tiendas**	**Shops**
sale el autobús?	does the bus leave?	el banco	bank
abre …?	does …open?	el estanco	tobacconist's
¿Hay visitas guiadas?	Are there guided tours?	la cafetería	café
¿Me puede recomendar …?	Can you recommend …?	la carnicería	butcher's
		la estación de trenes	train station
un restaurante típico	a typical restaurant	la farmacia	pharmacy / chemist
un hotel / una excursión	a hotel / a trip	la frutería	greengrocer's
		la joyería	jeweller's
Had a look ☐ **Nearly there** ☐ **Nailed it** ☐		la librería	book shop
¿Qué haremos mañana?	What will we do tomorrow?	la panadería	bakery
		la papelería	stationery shop
Sacaré muchas fotos.	I will take lots of photos.	la pastelería	cake shop
Subiremos al teleférico.	We will go up on the cable car.	la peluquería	hairdresser's
		la pescadería	fish shop
Bajaremos a pie.	We will go down on foot.	la tienda de ropa	clothes shop
Pasaremos entre las nubes.	We will go through the clouds.	la zapatería	shoe shop
		Had a look ☐ **Nearly there** ☐ **Nailed it** ☐	
Iremos a la playa / a la montaña / de excursión en barco.	We will go to the beach / to the mountains / on a boat trip.	un regalo	a present
		sellos	stamps
Haremos piragüismo.	We will go canoeing.	una carta / unas cartas	a letter / a few letters
Podremos hacer paddlesurf.	We will be able to go paddlesurfing.	recoger	to pick up
		mandar	to send
Podrás comprar regalos.	You will be able to buy presents.	horario comercial / horas de apertura	business hours / opening hours
será genial / mejor nos llevará	it will be great / better he/she will take us	de lunes a viernes	from Monday to Friday

29

Módulo 5 Palabras

abre a la(s) … / cierra a la(s) …	it opens at … / it closes at …
no cierra a mediodía	it doesn't close at midday
cerrado domingos y festivos	closed on Sundays and public holidays
abierto todos los días	open every day

Had a look ☐ **Nearly there** ☐ **Nailed it** ☐

Recuerdos y regalos — Souvenirs and presents

el abanico	fan
el chorizo	chorizo (sausage)
el llavero	key ring
el oso de peluche	teddy bear
los pendientes	earrings
la gorra	cap
la taza	mug
las golosinas	sweets
las pegatinas	stickers
¿Me puede ayudar?	Can you help me?
Quiero comprar …	I want to buy …
¿Tiene uno/a/os/as más barato/a/os/as?	Do you have a cheaper one / cheaper ones?
un billete de (cincuenta) euros	a (fifty) euro note
Tengo cambio.	I have change.

Had a look ☐ **Nearly there** ☐ **Nailed it** ☐

Quejas — Complaints

Quiero devolver …	I want to return …
está roto/a	it is broken
es demasiado estrecho/a / largo/a	it is too tight / long
tiene un agujero / una mancha	it has a hole / a stain
falta un botón	it's missing a button
¿Puede reembolsarme (el dinero)?	Can you reimburse me (the money)?
Podemos hacer un cambio.	We can exchange (it).
¿Qué me recomienda?	What do you recommend?
¿Qué tal …? / ¿Qué te parece(n) …?	What about …? / What do you think of …?
Te queda bien.	It suits you.
Te quedan demasiado grandes.	They are too big for you.
una talla más grande / pequeña	a bigger / smaller size
en rebajas	on sale
Me lo/la/los/las llevo.	I'll take it / them.

Had a look ☐ **Nearly there** ☐ **Nailed it** ☐

De compras — Shopping

Normalmente voy … / Suelo ir …	Usually I go … / I tend to go …
a los centros comerciales	to shopping centres
de tiendas con mis amigos	shopping with my friends
Nunca me ha gustado / Prefiero / Odio …	I've never liked / I prefer / I hate …
comprar en …	shopping in …
cadenas / grandes almacenes	chain stores / department stores
tiendas de diseño / segunda mano	designer shops / second-hand shops
comprar por Internet / en la red	shopping on the internet / online
hacer cola	queueing
porque …	because …
es más económico / práctico / cómodo	it's cheaper / more practical / more convenient
es un buen sitio para pasar la tarde	it's a good place for spending the afternoon
hay más variedad / demasiada gente	there is more variety / there are too many people
los precios son más bajos	the prices are lower
hay más ofertas	there are more offers
ropa alternativa / de moda	alternative clothing / fashionable clothing
gangas	bargains
artículos de marca	branded items

Had a look ☐ **Nearly there** ☐ **Nailed it** ☐

Los pros y los contras de la ciudad — The for and against of living in a city

Lo mejor de vivir en la ciudad es que …	The best thing about living in a city is that …
es tan fácil desplazarse	it's so easy to get around
hay una red de transporte público	there is a public transport system
hay tantas diversiones	there are so many things to do
hay muchas posibilidades de trabajo	there are lots of job opportunities
Lo peor es que …	The worst thing is that …
el centro es tan ruidoso	the centre is so noisy
hay tanto tráfico / tantos coches	there is so much traffic / so many cars
se lleva una vida tan frenética	life is so frenetic
la gente no se conoce	people don't know each other
En el campo …	In the countryside …
el transporte público no es fiable	public transport is not reliable
hay bastante desempleo	there is quite a lot of unemployment
no hay tantos atascos como antes	there are not as many traffic jams as before
yo conozco a todos mis vecinos	I know all my neighbours

Had a look ☐ **Nearly there** ☐ **Nailed it** ☐

Módulo 5 Palabras

¿Qué harías?	*What would you do?*
Introduciría más zonas peatonales.	*I would introduce more pedestrian areas.*
Renovaría … algunos edificios antiguos	*I would renovate … some old buildings*
las zonas deterioradas en las afueras	*the dilapidated areas on the outskirts*
Mejoraría el sistema de transporte.	*I would improve the transport system.*
Pondría / Crearía más áreas de ocio.	*I would put in / create more leisure areas.*
Construiría un nuevo centro comercial.	*I would build a new shopping centre.*
Invertiría en el turismo rural.	*I would invest in rural tourism.*
Controlaría el ruido.	*I would limit the noise.*

Had a look ☐ **Nearly there** ☐ **Nailed it** ☐

Destino Arequipa	*Destination Arequipa*
Vi / Vimos lugares interesantes.	*I saw / We saw interesting places.*
Tuvimos un guía.	*We had a guide.*
Nos hizo un recorrido.	*He/She did a tour for us.*
Nos ayudó a entender toda la historia.	*He/She helped us to understand all of the history.*
Recorrí a pie el centro histórico.	*I walked around the historic centre.*
Compré tantas cosas.	*I bought so many things.*
Alquilé una bici de montaña.	*I hired a mountain bike.*
Cogí un autobús turístico.	*I took a tourist bus.*
subimos / bajamos	*we went up / we went down*
Aprendí mucho sobre la cultura.	*I learned a lot about the culture.*
Me quedé impresionado con la ciudad.	*I was really impressed by the city.*
Había vistas maravillosas.	*There were amazing views.*
La comida estaba muy buena.	*The food was very good.*
La gente era abierta.	*The people were open.*
Lo que más me gustó fue / fueron …	*What I liked most was / were …*
¡Fue una experiencia única!	*It was a one-off experience!*
¡Qué miedo!	*What a scare!*
Volveré algún día.	*I will go back one day.*
Aprenderé a hacer surf.	*I will learn to surf.*
Trabajaré como voluntario/a.	*I will work as a volunteer.*

Had a look ☐ **Nearly there** ☐ **Nailed it** ☐

M5

31

Módulo 5 Palabras

Extra words I should know for reading and listening activities

¿Qué tiempo hace?
¿Qué tiempo* hace en …?
está despejado
la niebla
lluvioso
el pronóstico del tiempo
Siempre hace buen tiempo en …
una ola de calor

What's the weather like?
What's the weather like in …?
it's fine / it's cloudless
fog
rainy
the weather forecast
The weather is / It's always fine in …
a heat wave

Had a look ☐   Nearly there ☐   Nailed it ☐

De compras
¿Qué talla tiene?
¿De qué color?
¿Cuánto es / son?
Aquí tiene. (formal)
el cinturón de cuero
el recibo
la falda
le falta un botón
económico/a

Shopping
What size are you?
What colour?
How much is it / are they?
Here you are. (polite)
leather belt
receipt
skirt
a button is missing
economical

Had a look ☐   Nearly there ☐   Nailed it ☐

¿Cómo es tu zona?
árabe
judío/a
romano/a
el barrio
la calle estrecha
la calleja
la cordillera
la cumbre
el ambiente urbano
el espectáculo ecuestre
el paraíso
el teleférico
el imán

What's your area like?
Arabic
Jewish
Roman
neighbourhood
narrow street
narrow street / alley
mountain range
top (of a mountain)
the urban environment
equestrian show
paradise
cable car
magnet

Had a look ☐   Nearly there ☐   Nailed it ☐

Verbos útiles
bajar a pie
caminar
contemplar las vistas
esquiar
han mejorado / introducido / renovado / construido / creado / plantado / abierto
madrugar
merecer la pena
probarse (ropa)
regresar
tener prisa

Useful verbs
to walk down (a mountain)
to walk (in the countryside)
to contemplate the views
to ski / to go skiing
they have improved / introduced / renovated / built / created / planted / opened
to get up early
to be worthwhile
to try on (clothes)
to return
to be in a hurry

Had a look ☐   Nearly there ☐   Nailed it ☐

Otras expresiones y palabras
a primera hora
buen ojo para los negocios
el empleo
gratis
la hora de descansar
Me quedé dormido/a.
Me quedé enamorado/a de la ciudad.
Me quedé sin palabras.
una pérdida de tiempo
testarudo/a como una mula**
el/la urbanita

Other expressions and words
first thing in the day
a good eye for business
employment
free (no charge)
time to have a rest
I fell asleep.
I fell in love with the city.
I was speechless.
a waste of time
as stubborn as a mule
city lover

Had a look ☐   Nearly there ☐   Nailed it ☐

⭐ ***Watch out for false friends**
Although *tiempo* can sometimes mean 'time', for example, *No tengo tiempo para hacer mis deberes* (I haven't got time to do my homework) in the question ¿Qué tiempo hace en …? it means 'weather'. To ask what time it is you say: ¿Qué **hora** es?

⭐ ****Try to work out the meaning of words you don't know**
Testarudo como una mula is a simile that you can translate directly into English. You only need to change one letter of *mula* to come up with 'mule' and you can then work out that *testarudo* must mean 'stubborn'.

Words I should know for speaking and writing activities

Las comidas	***Meals***
el desayuno	*breakfast*
la comida / el almuerzo	*lunch*
la merienda	*tea (meal)*
la cena	*dinner / evening meal*
desayunar	*to have breakfast / to have ... for breakfast*
comer / almorzar	*to have lunch / to have ... for lunch*
merendar	*to have tea / to have ... for tea*
cenar	*to have dinner / to have ... for dinner*
tomar	*to have (food / drink)*
beber	*to drink*
entre semana ...	*during the week ...*
los fines de semana ...	*at weekends ...*
Desayuno a las ocho.	*I have breakfast at eight o'clock.*
Desayuno / Como / Meriendo / Ceno ...	*For breakfast / lunch / tea / dinner I have ...*
un huevo	*an egg*

Had a look ☐ **Nearly there** ☐ **Nailed it** ☐

un yogur	*a yogurt*
un pastel	*a cake*
un bocadillo	*a sandwich*
una hamburguesa	*a hamburger*
(el) café / (el) té	*coffee / tea*
(el) Cola Cao	*Cola Cao (Spanish hot chocolate drink)*
(el) marisco	*seafood*
(el) pescado	*fish*
(el) pollo	*chicken*
(el) zumo de naranja	*orange juice*
(la) carne	*meat*
(la) ensalada	*salad*

Had a look ☐ **Nearly there** ☐ **Nailed it** ☐

(la) fruta	*fruit*
(la) leche	*milk*
(la) sopa	*soup*
(la) tortilla	*omelette*
(los) cereales	*cereals*
(los) churros	*fried doughnut sticks*
(las) galletas	*biscuits*
(las) patatas fritas	*chips*
(las) tostadas	*toast*
(las) verduras	*vegetables*
algo dulce / ligero / rápido	*something sweet / light / quick*
ser goloso/a	*to have a sweet tooth*
tener hambre	*to be hungry*
tener prisa	*to be in a hurry*

tomar un desayuno fuerte	*to have a big (lit. strong) breakfast*

Had a look ☐ **Nearly there** ☐ **Nailed it** ☐

Las expresiones de cantidad	***Expressions of quantity***
cien / quinientos gramos de ...	*100 / 500 grammes of ...*
un bote de ...	*a jar of ...*
un kilo de ...	*a kilo of ...*
un litro de ...	*a litre of ...*
un paquete de ...	*a packet of ...*
una barra de ...	*a loaf of ...*
una botella de ...	*a bottle of ...*
una caja de ...	*a box of ...*
una docena de ...	*a dozen ...*
una lata de ...	*a tin / can of ...*

Had a look ☐ **Nearly there** ☐ **Nailed it** ☐

Los alimentos	***Food products***
el aceite de oliva	*olive oil*
el agua	*water*
el ajo	*garlic*
el arroz	*rice*
el atún	*tuna*
el azúcar	*sugar*
el chorizo	*spicy sausage*
el maíz	*corn*
el pan	*bread*
el queso	*cheese*
la cerveza	*beer*
la carne de cerdo / cordero / ternera	*pork / lamb / beef*
la coliflor	*cauliflower*
la harina	*flour*
la mantequilla	*butter*
la mermelada	*jam*
los albaricoques	*apricots*
los guisantes	*peas*
los lácteos	*dairy products*
los melocotones	*peaches*

Had a look ☐ **Nearly there** ☐ **Nailed it** ☐

los melones	*melons*
los pepinos	*cucumbers*
los pimientos	*peppers*
los plátanos	*bananas*
los pomelos	*grapefruits*
los refrescos	*fizzy drinks*
las cebollas	*onions*
las fresas	*strawberries*
las judías (verdes)	*(green) beans*
las legumbres	*pulses*
las lentejas	*lentils*

Módulo 6 Palabras

las manzanas	apples
las naranjas	oranges
las peras	pears
las piñas	pineapples
las uvas	grapes
las zanahorias	carrots

Had a look ☐ **Nearly there** ☐ **Nailed it** ☐

¿Has probado …?	Have you tried …?
el gazpacho	gazpacho (chilled soup)
la ensaladilla rusa	Russian salad
la fabada	stew of beans and pork
Es un tipo de bebida / postre.	It's a type of drink / dessert.
Es un plato caliente / frío.	It's a hot / cold dish.
Contiene(n) …	It contains / They contain …
Fue inventado/a / introducido/a …	It was invented / introduced …

Had a look ☐ **Nearly there** ☐ **Nailed it** ☐

Mi rutina diaria — My daily routine

me despierto	I wake up
me levanto	I get up
me ducho	I have a shower
me peino	I brush my hair
me afeito	I have a shave
me visto	I get dressed
me lavo los dientes	I clean my teeth
me acuesto	I go to bed
salgo de casa	I leave home
vuelvo a casa	I return home
temprano / tarde	early / late
enseguida	straight away
odio levantarme	I hate getting up

Had a look ☐ **Nearly there** ☐ **Nailed it** ☐

¿Qué le pasa? — What's the matter?

No me encuentro bien.	I don't feel well.
Me siento fatal.	I feel awful.
Estoy enfermo/a / cansado/a.	I am ill / tired.
Tengo calor / frío.	I am hot / cold.
Tengo catarro.	I have a cold.
Tengo diarrea.	I have diarrhoea.
Tengo dolor de cabeza.	I have a headache.
Tengo fiebre.	I have a fever / temperature.
Tengo gripe.	I have flu.
Tengo mucho sueño.	I am very sleepy.
Tengo náuseas.	I feel sick.
Tengo quemaduras de sol.	I have sunburn.
Tengo tos.	I have a cough.
Tengo una insolación.	I have sunstroke.
Tengo una picadura.	I've been stung.

Had a look ☐ **Nearly there** ☐ **Nailed it** ☐

Me duele(n) …	My … hurt(s).
Me he cortado el/la …	I've cut my …
Me he hecho daño en …	I've hurt my …
Me he quemado …	I've burnt my …
Me he roto …	I've broken my …
Me he torcido …	I've twisted my …
el brazo / el estómago	arm / stomach
el pie / el tobillo	foot / ankle
la boca / la cabeza	mouth / head
la espalda / la garganta	back / throat
la mano / la nariz	hand / nose
la pierna / la rodilla	leg / knee
los dientes / las muelas	teeth
los oídos / las orejas	ears
los ojos	eyes

Had a look ☐ **Nearly there** ☐ **Nailed it** ☐

¿Desde hace cuánto tiempo?	How long for?
desde hace …	for …
un día / un mes	a day / a month
una hora / una semana	an hour / a week
¿Desde cuándo?	Since when?
desde ayer	since yesterday
desde anteayer	since the day before yesterday
no se preocupe	don't worry
¡Qué mala suerte!	What bad luck!
Tiene(s) que / Hay que …	You have to …
beber mucha agua	drink lots of water
descansar	rest
ir al hospital / médico / dentista	go to the hospital / doctor / dentist
tomar aspirinas	take aspirins
tomar este jarabe / estas pastillas	take this syrup / these tablets
usar esta crema	use this cream

Had a look ☐ **Nearly there** ☐ **Nailed it** ☐

Las fiestas — Festivals

la fiesta de …	the festival of …
esta tradición antigua …	this old tradition …
se caracteriza por …	is characterised by …
se celebra en …	is celebrated in …
se repite …	is repeated …
se queman figuras de madera	wooden figures are burnt
se construyen hogueras	bonfires are built
se disparan fuegos artificiales	fireworks are set off
se lanzan huevos	eggs are thrown
las calles se llenan de …	the streets are filled with …
los niños / los jóvenes …	children / young people …
los familiares / las familias …	relations / families …
comen manzanas de caramelo	eat toffee apples

Módulo 6 Palabras

decoran las casas / las tumbas con flores / velas	decorate houses / graves with flowers / candles
preparan linternas / altares	prepare lanterns / altars
se disfrazan de brujas / fantasmas	dress up as witches / ghosts
ven desfiles	watch processions

Had a look ☐ Nearly there ☐ Nailed it ☐

Un día especial — A special day

Abrimos los regalos.	We open the presents.
Buscamos huevos de chocolate.	We look for chocolate eggs.
Cantamos villancicos.	We sing Christmas carols.
Cenamos bacalao.	We have cod for dinner.
Comemos dulces navideños / doce uvas / pavo.	We eat Christmas sweets / twelve grapes / turkey.
Nos acostamos muy tarde.	We go to bed very late.
Nos levantamos muy temprano.	We get up very early.
Rezamos.	We pray.
Vamos a la mezquita / iglesia.	We go to the mosque / church.
Ayer fue …	Yesterday was …
el baile de fin de curso	the school prom
el Día de Navidad	Christmas Day
(el) Domingo de Pascua	Easter Sunday
(la) Nochebuena	Christmas Eve
(la) Nochevieja	New Year's Eve
Me bañé y luego me maquillé.	I had a bath and then did my make-up.

Had a look ☐ Nearly there ☐ Nailed it ☐

¿Qué va a tomar? — What are you going to have?

de primer / segundo plato …	for starter / main course …
de postre …	for dessert …
Voy a tomar …	I'm going to have …
(el) bistec	steak
(el) filete de cerdo	pork fillet
(el) flan	crème caramel
(el) jamón serrano	Serrano ham
(la) merluza en salsa verde	hake in parsley and wine sauce
(la) sopa de fideos	noodle soup
(la) tortilla de espinacas	spinach omelette
(la) trucha a la plancha	grilled trout
(los) calamares	squid
(las) albóndigas	meatballs
(las) chuletas de cordero asadas	roast lamb chops
(las) croquetas caseras	home-made croquettes
(las) gambas	prawns
(las) natillas	custard

Had a look ☐ Nearly there ☐ Nailed it ☐

¿Qué me recomienda?	What do you recommend?
el menú del día	the set menu
la especialidad de la casa	the house speciality
está buenísimo/a / riquísimo/a	is extremely good / tasty
¡Que aproveche!	Enjoy your meal!
¿Algo más?	Anything else?
Nada más, gracias.	Nothing else, thank you.
¿Me trae la cuenta, por favor?	Can you bring me the bill, please?
No tengo cuchillo / tenedor / cuchara.	I haven't got a knife / fork / spoon.
No hay aceite / sal / vinagre.	There's no oil / salt / vinegar.
El plato / vaso / mantel está sucio.	The plate / glass / table cloth is dirty.
El vino está malo.	The wine is bad / off.
La carne está fría.	The meat is cold.
dejar una propina	to leave a tip
equivocarse	to make a mistake
pedir	to order / to ask for
ser alérgico/a …	to be allergic to …
ser vegetariano/a	to be a vegetarian

Had a look ☐ Nearly there ☐ Nailed it ☐

Un festival de música — A music festival

Me fascina(n) …	…fascinate(s) me.
Admiro …	I admire …
No aguanto / soporto …	I can't stand …
su actitud / talento	his/her attitude / talent
su comportamiento	his/her behaviour
su determinación / estilo	his/her determination / style
su forma de vestir	his/her way of dressing
su música / voz	his/her music / voice
sus canciones / coreografías	his/her songs / choreography
sus ideas / letras	his/her ideas / lyrics
atrevido/a(s)	daring
imaginativo/a(s)	imaginative
precioso/a(s)	beautiful
repetitivo/a(s)	repetitive
original(es)	original
triste(s)	sad
Me/Te hace(n) falta …	I/You need …
crema solar	sun cream
el pasaporte / DNI	your passport / national ID card
un sombrero / una gorra	a hat / cap

Had a look ☐ Nearly there ☐ Nailed it ☐

M6

35

Módulo 6 Palabras

Extra words I should know for reading and listening activities

Verbos y expresiones útiles	Useful verbs and expressions
prestar atención	to pay attention
romperse (el brazo)*	to break (your arm)
torcerse (el tobillo)*	to twist (your ankle)
sentirse mal	to feel bad / to not feel very well
hacerse daño	to hurt yourself
doblar servilletas	to fold serviettes
atraer	to attract
sufrir accidentes domésticos	to have domestic accidents
concienciar	to raise awareness
aprobar	to approve
montar una tienda	to put up a tent
sin contar	not counting
Estas gambas están buenísimas.**	These prawns are extremely good.
No me quedé nada decepcionado/a.	I wasn't at all disappointed.

Had a look ☐ Nearly there ☐ Nailed it ☐

Alimentos y comidas	Food products and meals
Apto para alérgicos / celiacos e intolerancias alimentarias.	Suitable for people with allergies / reactions / celiacs and food intolerances.
el asado de pavo	roast turkey dinner
el bufé libre	self-service buffet
la comida rápida / sencilla de preparar	fast / convenience food
las delicias culinarias	culinary treats
la dieta mediterránea / equilibrada / sana	Mediterranean / balanced / healthy diet
el guiso	stew
el horno	oven
la intoxicación alimentaria	food poisoning
los mazapanes	marzipan sweets

Had a look ☐ Nearly there ☐ Nailed it ☐

⭐ *Use the definite article to say you have hurt / broken / twisted / cut or burned something

In Spanish the definite article *el* or *la* is used with verbs such as *romperse* (to break), *torcerse* (to twist), *doler* (to hurt), *cortarse* (to cut oneself) and *quemarse* (to burn oneself), for example:
Me he roto la pierna. → I've broken **my** leg.
Se ha torcido el tobillo. → He/She has twisted **her** ankle.
Me duele la cabeza. → **My** head aches.
Note too that *doler* is a stem-changing word and *romperse* an irregular verb — the past participle is *roto*.

Fiestas y celebraciones	Festivals and celebrations
acceso para minusválidos	wheelchair access
el belén	nativity scene
las bodas de plata	silver wedding
la calavera	skull
la campanada	stroke of the bell
el DNI (Documento Nacional de Identidad)	identity card
la edad mínima	minimum age
el encierro	bull running
el fracaso de la conspiración de la pólvora	gunpower plot
las luces navideñas	Christmas lights
la medianoche	midnight
la muñeca	doll
el peligro	danger
los poseedores de abono de 2 / 3 o 4 días	those who have a ticket for 2 / 3 or 4 days
la pulsera	bracelet
la quinceañera	15-year-old girl (in Latin American countries they have a big celebration when a girl turns 15)
los seres queridos	loved ones
el sinfín	endless number
el tintineo	ringing (of mobile phone)
truco o trato	trick or treat
la población indígena	the indigenous population

Had a look ☐ Nearly there ☐ Nailed it ☐

Adjetivos útiles	Useful adjectives
sabroso/a	tasty
picante / salado/a	spicy / salty
asqueroso/a	disgusting
orgulloso/a	proud
torpe	clumsy
encantador(a)	charming
al ajillo	cooked with garlic
andino/a	Andean
caribeño/a	Caribbean
ubicado/a	situated
compuesto/a de ...	which has ... in it

Had a look ☐ Nearly there ☐ Nailed it ☐

⭐ **How to make adjectives stronger
To say really (nice), extremely (expensive), etc. add *–ísimo* to the end of the adjective, and make it agree, for example, *Este ejercicio es facilísimo* (This exercise is really easy). If the adjective ends in a vowel, remove the vowel before adding the ending, so, for example, *bueno* becomes *buenísimo* and *importante* becomes *importantísimo*.

Words I should know for speaking and writing activities

¿En qué trabajas?	What is your job?
Soy … / Es …	I am … / He/She is …
Me gustaría ser …	I would like to be a…
abogado/a	lawyer
albañil	bricklayer / builder
amo/a de casa	househusband / housewife
azafato/a	flight attendant
bailarín / bailarina	dancer
bombero/a	firefighter
camarero/a	waiter / waitress
cantante	singer
cocinero/a	cook
contable	accountant
dependiente/a	shop assistant
diseñador(a)	designer

Had a look ☐ **Nearly there** ☐ **Nailed it** ☐

electricista	electrician
enfermero/a	nurse
escritor(a)	writer
fontanero/a	plumber
fotógrafo/a	photographer
funcionario/a	civil servant
guía turístico/a	tour guide
ingeniero/a	engineer
jardinero/a	gardener
mecánico/a	mechanic
médico/a	doctor
músico/a	musician
peluquero/a	hairdresser
periodista	journalist
policía	police officer
profesor(a)	teacher
recepcionista	receptionist
socorrista	lifeguard
soldado	soldier
veterinario/a	vet

Had a look ☐ **Nearly there** ☐ **Nailed it** ☐

Es un trabajo …	It's a … job
artístico / emocionante	artistic / exciting
exigente / importante	demanding / important
fácil / difícil	easy / difficult
manual / monótono	manual / monotonous
variado / repetitivo	varied / repetitive
con responsabilidad	with responsibility
con buenas perspectivas	with good prospects
con un buen sueldo	with a good salary

Had a look ☐ **Nearly there** ☐ **Nailed it** ☐

Tengo que … / Suelo …	I have to … / I tend to …
cuidar a los clientes / pacientes / pasajeros	look after the customers / patients / passengers
contestar llamadas telefónicas	answer telephone calls
cuidar las plantas y las flores	look after the plants and flowers
enseñar / vigilar a los niños	teach / supervise the children
hacer entrevistas	do interviews
preparar platos distintos	prepare different dishes
reparar coches	repair cars
servir comida y bebida	serve food and drink
trabajar en un taller / en un hospital / en una tienda / a bordo de un avión	work in a workshop / in a hospital / in a shop / aboard a plane
vender ropa de marca	sell designer clothing
viajar por todo el mundo	travel the world

Had a look ☐ **Nearly there** ☐ **Nailed it** ☐

¿Qué tipo de persona eres?	What type of person are you?
Creo que soy …	I think I'm …
ambicioso/a	ambitious
comprensivo/a	understanding
creativo/a	creative
extrovertido/a	extroverted / outgoing
fuerte	strong
inteligente	intelligent
organizado/a	organised
paciente	patient
práctico/a	practical
serio/a	serious
trabajador(a)	hardworking
valiente	brave

Had a look ☐ **Nearly there** ☐ **Nailed it** ☐

¿Qué haces para ganar dinero?	What do you do to earn money?
¿Tienes un trabajo a tiempo parcial?	Do you have a part-time job?
Reparto periódicos.	I deliver newspapers.
Hago de canguro.	I babysit.
Trabajo de cajero/a.	I work as a cashier.
Ayudo con las tareas domésticas.	I help with the housework.
Cocino.	I cook.
Lavo los platos.	I wash the dishes.
Paso la aspiradora.	I do the vacuuming.
Plancho la ropa.	I iron the clothes.
Pongo y quito la mesa.	I lay and clear the table.
Paseo al perro.	I walk the dog.
Corto el césped.	I cut the lawn.

Had a look ☐ **Nearly there** ☐ **Nailed it** ☐

Lo hago …	I do it …
los sábados	on Saturdays
antes / después del insti	before / after school
cuando necesito dinero	when I need money

Módulo 7 Palabras

cuando mi madre está trabajando	when my mum is working
cuando me necesitan	when they need me
cada mañana	each / every morning
una vez / dos veces a la semana	once / twice a week
Gano ... euros / libras a la hora / al día / a la semana.	I earn ... euros / pounds per hour / day / week.
Me llevo bien con mis compañeros.	I get on well with my colleagues.
Mi jefe/a es amable.	My boss is nice.
El horario es flexible.	The hours are flexible.

Had a look ☐ Nearly there ☐ Nailed it ☐

Mis prácticas laborales / Work experience

Hice mis prácticas laborales en ...	I did my work experience in ...
Pasé quince días trabajando en ...	I spent a fortnight working in ...
un polideportivo	a sports centre
una agencia de viajes / una granja	a travel agency / a farm
una escuela / una oficina	a school / an office
una fábrica de juguetes	a toy factory
una tienda benéfica / solidaria	a charity shop
la empresa de mi madre	my mum's company

Had a look ☐ Nearly there ☐ Nailed it ☐

El primer / último día conocí a / llegué ...	On the first / last day I met / I arrived ...
Cada día / Todos los días ...	Each / Every day ...
archivaba documentos	I filed documents
ayudaba ...	I helped ...
cogía el autobús / el metro	I caught the bus / underground
empezaba / terminaba a las ...	I started / finished at ...
hacía una variedad de tareas	I did a variety of tasks
iba en transporte público	I went by public transport
llevaba ropa elegante	I wore smart clothes
ponía folletos en los estantes	I put brochures on the shelves
sacaba fotocopias	I did photocopying

Had a look ☐ Nearly there ☐ Nailed it ☐

Mi jefe/a era ...	My boss was ...
Mis compañeros eran ...	My colleagues were ...
Los clientes eran ...	The customers were ...
alegre(s)	cheerful
(des)agradable(s)	(un)pleasant
(mal)educado/a(s)	polite (rude)
El trabajo era duro.	The job was hard.
Aprendí ... muchas nuevas habilidades	I learned ... lots of new skills
a trabajar en equipo	to work in a team
a usar ...	to use ...
No aprendí nada nuevo.	I didn't learn anything new.

Had a look ☐ Nearly there ☐ Nailed it ☐

¿Por qué aprender idiomas? / Why learn languages?

Aumenta tu confianza.	It increases your confidence.
Estimula el cerebro.	It stimulates the brain.
Mejora tus perspectivas laborales.	It improves your job prospects.
Te abre la mente.	It opens your mind.
Te hace parecer más atractivo.	It makes you appear more attractive.
Te ayuda a ...	It helps you to ...
Te permite ...	It allows you to ...
apreciar la vida cultural de otros países	appreciate the cultural life of other countries
conocer a mucha gente distinta	meet lots of different people
conocer nuevos sitios	get to know new places
encontrar un trabajo	find a job
descubrir nuevas culturas	discover new cultures
establecer buenas relaciones	establish good relationships
hacer nuevos amigos	make new friends
mejorar tu lengua materna	improve your first language
solucionar problemas	solve problems
trabajar o estudiar en el extranjero	work or study abroad
Me hace falta saber hablar idiomas extranjeros.	I need to know how to speak foreign languages.
(No) Domino el inglés.	I (don't) speak English fluently.
Hablo un poco de ruso.	I speak a bit of Russian.

Had a look ☐ Nearly there ☐ Nailed it ☐

Solicitando un trabajo / Applying for a job

Se busca / Se requiere ...	... required.
(No) Hace falta experiencia.	Experience (not) needed.
Muy señor mío	Dear Sir
Le escribo para solicitar el puesto de ...	I'm writing to apply for the post of ...
Le adjunto mi currículum vitae.	I'm enclosing my CV.
Le agradezco su amable atención.	Thank you for your kind attention.
Atentamente	Yours sincerely / faithfully

Módulo 7 Palabras

Me apetece trabajar en …	Working in … appeals to me.
(No) Tengo experiencia previa.	I (don't) have previous experience.
He estudiado / trabajado …	I've studied / worked …
He hecho un curso de …	I've done a course in …
Tengo …	I have …
buen sentido del humor	a good sense of humour
buenas capacidades de comunicación / resolución de problemas	good communication / problem-solving skills
buenas habilidades lingüísticas	good language skills

Had a look ☐ Nearly there ☐ Nailed it ☐

Un año sabático / A gap year

Si pudiera tomarme un año sabático …	If I could take a gap year …
Si tuviera bastante dinero …	If I had enough money …
apoyaría un proyecto medioambiental	I would support an environmental project
aprendería a esquiar	I would learn to ski
ayudaría a construir un colegio	I would help to build a school
buscaría un trabajo	I would look for a job
enseñaría inglés	I would teach English
ganaría mucho dinero	I would earn a lot of money
haría un viaje en Interrail	I would go Interrailing
iría a España / donde …	I would go to Spain / where …
mejoraría mi nivel de español	I would improve my level of Spanish
nunca olvidaría la experiencia	I would never forget the experience
pasaría un año en …	I would spend a year in …
trabajaría en un orfanato	I would work in an orphanage
viajaría con mochila por el mundo	I would go backpacking around the world

Had a look ☐ Nearly there ☐ Nailed it ☐

¿Cómo viajarías? / How would you travel?

Cogería el / Viajaría en autobús / autocar / avión / tren.	I would catch the / travel by bus / coach / plane / train.
Es más barato / cómodo / rápido.	It's cheaper / more comfortable / quicker.
Puedes …	You can …
ver vídeos mientras viajas	watch videos whilst you travel
dejar tu maleta en la consigna	leave your suitcase in the left-luggage office
Hay muchos / pocos atascos / retrasos …	There are lots of / few traffic jams / delays …
en las autopistas / las carreteras	on the motorways / roads
Los billetes son carísimos.	The tickets are extremely expensive.
Los conductores están en huelga.	The drivers are on strike.
Odio esperar en la parada de autobús.	I hate waiting at the bus stop.
Tengo miedo a volar.	I'm scared of flying.

Had a look ☐ Nearly there ☐ Nailed it ☐

Viajando en tren / Travelling by train

El tren con destino a … efectuará su salida … de la vía / del andén dos	The train to … will leave / depart … from platform two
el (tren) AVE	high-speed train
la taquilla	the ticket office
Quisiera un billete de ida a …	I would like a single ticket to …
Quisiera un billete de ida y vuelta a …	I would like a return ticket to …
¿De qué andén sale?	From which platform does it leave?
¿A qué hora sale / llega?	What time does it leave / arrive?
¿Es directo o hay que cambiar?	Is it direct or do I have to change?

Had a look ☐ Nearly there ☐ Nailed it ☐

El futuro / The future

Me interesa(n) …	…interest(s) me.
Me importa(n) …	…matter(s) to me.
Me preocupa(n) …	…worry / worries me.
el desempleo / el paro	unemployment
el dinero / el éxito	money / success
el fracaso / el matrimonio	failure / marriage
la responsabilidad	responsibility
la independencia / la pobreza	independence / poverty
los niños / las notas	children / marks
Espero …	I hope to …
Me gustaría …	I would like to …
Pienso …	I plan to / intend to …
Quiero …	I want to …
Tengo la intención de …	I intend to …
Voy a …	I am going to …

Had a look ☐ Nearly there ☐ Nailed it ☐

aprender a conducir	learn to drive
aprobar mis exámenes	pass my exams
casarme	get married
conseguir un buen empleo / trabajo	get a good job
estudiar una carrera universitaria	study a university course
montar mi propio negocio	set up my own business

M 7

39

Módulo 7 Palabras

sacar buenas notas	get good marks
ser feliz	be happy
tener hijos	have children
trabajar como voluntario/a	work as a volunteer
Cuando …	When …
gane bastante dinero …	I earn enough money …
me enamore …	I fall in love …
sea mayor …	I'm older …
tenga … años …	I'm … years old …
vaya a la universidad …	I go to university …
termine este curso / el bachillerato / la formación profesional / la licenciatura …	I finish this course / my A Levels / my vocational course / my degree …
buscaré un trabajo	I will look for a job
compartiré piso con …	I will share a flat with …
compraré un coche / una casa	I will buy a car / house
iré a otro insti / a la universidad	I will go to another school / to university
me casaré	I will get married
me iré de casa	I will leave home
seguiré estudiando en mi insti	I will carry on studying at my school
seré famoso/a	I will be famous
me tomaré un año sabático	I will take a gap year
trabajaré como …	I will work as …

Had a look ☐ **Nearly there** ☐ **Nailed it** ☐

Módulo 7 Palabras

Extra words I should know for reading and listening activities

Verbos útiles	Useful verbs
ahorrar	to save (up)
alistarse en el ejército	to enlist in the army
aprovechar	to make the most of
arreglar (una habitación)	to tidy (a room)
barrer las hojas	to sweep up leaves
buscar un trabajo como …	to look for a job as a …
cortar el pelo	to cut hair
cumplir un sueño	to make a dream come true
descuidar	to neglect
obtener el título de	to qualify as …
estar harto/a de	to be fed up with
mantener el equilibrio	to maintain the balance
merecer / valer la pena	to be worthwhile
ordeñar (una vaca)	to milk (a cow)
quitar la nieve	to clear the snow
trabajar al aire libre	to work outside
viajar como mochilero/a*	to go backpacking

Had a look ☐   Nearly there ☐   Nailed it ☐

El mundo laboral	The world of work
el/la amo/a de casa	househusband / housewife
el/la animador(a)	events organiser / entertainer
el anuncio	advertisement
la antigüedad	number of years spent in a job
el/la corresponsal de guerra	war correspondent
el curso de formación	training course
el curso de primeros auxilios	first aid course
el curso optativo (de pastelería, etc.)	optional (pastry-making, etc.) course
el departamento de ventas	sales department
el descanso	break
la deuda	debt
la emisora de radio	radio station
el/la empleado/a	employee
la fiesta de despedida	farewell party

Had a look ☐   Nearly there ☐   Nailed it ☐

la gestión administrativa	business management
la hostelería	hotel industry
el/la ingeniero/a de sonido	sound engineer
la manera de vestir	the way you dress
el medio ambiente	the environment
el oficio	trade / profession
el paquete de beneficios	benefits package
las perspectivas	prospects
el plan de seguro médico	medical insurance
la reunión	meeting
un salario bajo / alto / justo	a low / high / fair wage / salary
la sanidad	health
la seguridad	safety
el trabajo de mis sueños	my dream job
el voluntariado	volunteering

Had a look ☐   Nearly there ☐   Nailed it ☐

Otras frases y palabras útiles	Other useful phrases and words
cariñoso/a	affectionate
cuando cumplas cinco años en la empresa	when you have worked for five years in the company
en referencia a	with reference to
experiencia deseable	experience desirable
honrado/a	honest
Me da la oportunidad de …	It gives me the chance to …
Me trataban como un esclavo.	They treated me like a slave.
No soporto a mi jefe.	I can't stand my boss.
¡Ojalá no fuera tan peligroso!	I wish it wasn't so dangerous.
salario a convenir	salary to be agreed
Serías un buen … / una buena …	You would be a good …
subvencionado/a	subsidised
¿Te apetece …?**	Do you fancy …?

Had a look ☐   Nearly there ☐   Nailed it ☐

> ⭐ ***Work out meanings of unfamiliar words**
> When trying to work out the meaning of a new word look for clues – think Context, Cognates, Common sense. For example, if you know the word *mochila* (backpack), you should be able to work out that *viajar como mochilero* would literally translate 'to travel as a backpacker'.

> ⭐ ****Memorise and adapt useful phrases**
> Learn useful phrases and adapt them to different contexts. You can use *¿Te apetece …?* to ask a friend what he or she would like to do.
> Example: *¿Te apetece ir al cine?* (Do you fancy going to the cinema?)
> And you could adapt it to say what you would fancy doing.
> Example: *Me apetece salir esta noche.* (I fancy going out tonight).

Words I should know for speaking and writing activities

¿Cómo es tu casa?	What is your house like?
Vivo en …	I live in …
un bloque de pisos	a block of flats
una casa individual	a detached house
una casa adosada	a semi-detached / terraced house
una residencia de ancianos	an old people's home
una finca / granja	a farmhouse
Alquilamos una casa amueblada.	We rent a furnished house.
Está en …	It is in / on …
un barrio de la ciudad	a district / suburb of the city / town
las afueras	the outskirts
el campo	the country
la costa	the coast
la montaña / sierra	the mountains
el cuarto piso de un edificio antiguo	the fourth floor of an old building

Had a look ☐ Nearly there ☐ Nailed it ☐

Mi apartamento / piso tiene …	My apartment / flat has …
tres dormitorios	three bedrooms
dos cuartos de baño	two bathrooms
una cocina amplia y bien equipada	a spacious / well-equipped kitchen
un comedor recién renovado	a recently refurbished dining room
un estudio	a study
un aseo	a toilet
un sótano	a basement / cellar
un salón	a living room
una mesa	a table
unas sillas	some chairs
Mi casa ideal sería …	My ideal house would be …
Tendría …	It would have …
una piscina climatizada	a heated swimming pool
mi propio cine en casa	my own home cinema
una sala de fiestas	a party room
Cambiaría los muebles.	I would change the furniture.
Pintaría … de otro color.	I would paint … another colour.

Had a look ☐ Nearly there ☐ Nailed it ☐

¿Cómo se debería cuidar el medio ambiente en casa?	How should you look after the environment at home?
Para cuidar el medio ambiente se debería …	To care for the environment you / one should …
apagar la luz	turn off the light
ducharse en vez de bañarse	have a shower instead of taking a bath
separar la basura	separate the rubbish
reciclar el plástico y el vidrio	recycle plastic and glass
desenchufar los aparatos eléctricos	unplug electric appliances
ahorrar energía	save energy
cerrar el grifo	turn off the tap
hacer todo lo posible	do everything possible
no se debería …	you / one should not …
malgastar el agua	waste water
usar bolsas de plástico	use plastic bags

Had a look ☐ Nearly there ☐ Nailed it ☐

¿Cuáles son los problemas globales más serios hoy en día?	What are the most serious global issues today?
Me preocupa(n) …	I am worried about …
el paro / desempleo	unemployment
el hambre / la pobreza	hunger / poverty
la deforestación	deforestation
la diferencia entre ricos y pobres	the difference between rich and poor
la drogadicción / la salud / la obesidad	drug addiction / health / obesity
la crisis económica	the economic crisis
los problemas del medio ambiente	environmental problems
los sin hogar / techo	the homeless
los animales en peligro de extinción	animals in danger of extinction

Had a look ☐ Nearly there ☐ Nailed it ☐

Es necesario / esencial que …	It's necessary / essential that (we) …
cuidemos el planeta	look after the planet
hagamos proyectos de conservación	do conservation projects
compremos / usemos productos verdes / de comercio justo	buy / use green / fairtrade products
apoyemos proyectos de ayuda	support aid projects
creemos oportunidades de trabajo	create job opportunities
ayudemos a evitar el consumo de sustancias perjudiciales	help to avoid the consumption of harmful substances
ahorremos agua	save water
construyamos más casas	build more houses
cambiemos la ley	change the law
consumamos menos	consume less
hagamos campañas publicitarias	carry out publicity campaigns

Módulo 8 Palabras

recaudemos dinero para organizaciones de caridad en el tercer mundo	raise money for charities in the third world
No es justo / Es terrible que haya …	It's not fair / It's terrible that there is …
tanta desigualdad social / contaminación	so much social inequality / pollution
tanta gente sin trabajo y sin techo	so many people out of work and homeless
tanta gente obesa y tantos drogadictos	so many obese people and so many drug addicts

Had a look ☐ Nearly there ☐ Nailed it ☐

¡Actúa localmente! / Act locally!

Hay demasiada …	There is / are too much / many …
basura en las calles	rubbish on the streets
gente sin espacio para vivir	people with nowhere to live
destrucción de los bosques	destruction of woodland / forest
polución de los mares y ríos	pollution of seas and rivers
El aire está contaminado.	The air is polluted.
Los combustibles fósiles se acaban.	Fossil fuels are running out.
No corte tantos árboles.	Don't cut down so many trees.
No vaya en coche si es posible ir a pie.	Don't go by car if it's possible to walk.
No tire basura al suelo.	Don't throw rubbish onto the ground.
No malgaste energía.	Don't waste energy.
No construya tantas casas grandes.	Don't build so many large houses.
No eche tantos desechos químicos.	Don't release so much chemical waste.
Plante más bosques y selvas.	Plant more woods and forests.
Reduzca las emisiones de los vehículos.	Reduce vehicle emissions.
Recicle el papel, el vidrio y el plástico.	Recycle paper, glass and plastic.
Use energías renovables.	Use renewable energies.
Diseñe casas más pequeñas.	Design smaller houses.
Introduzca leyes más estrictas.	Introduce stricter laws.

Had a look ☐ Nearly there ☐ Nailed it ☐

llevar una vida más verde	(to) live a greener life
salvar el planeta	(to) save the planet
reducir la huella de carbono	(to) reduce your carbon footprint
ecológico/a	environmentally-friendly
el techo	roof
el agua de lluvia	rain water
el domicilio	home
los recursos naturales	natural resources
los paneles solares	solar panels
la arena	sand
los (eco-)ladrillos	(eco-)bricks
una fábrica	a factory
mudarse (de casa)	(to) move house

Had a look ☐ Nearly there ☐ Nailed it ☐

Una dieta sana / A healthy diet

los alimentos	foods
lácteos	milk products
carne / pescados y huevos	meat / fish and eggs
frutas y verduras	fruit and vegetables
cereales	cereals
fideos	noodles
grasas	fats
dulces	sugars / sweet things
legumbres	pulses
frutos secos	nuts and dried fruit
los nutrientes	nutrients
proteínas	proteins
minerales	minerals
grasa	fat
sal	salt
vitaminas	vitamins
azúcar	sugar
gluten	gluten
el sabor	taste

Had a look ☐ Nearly there ☐ Nailed it ☐

vegetariano / vegano	vegetarian / vegan
saludable / sano / malsano	healthy / healthy / unhealthy
(No) Tengo hambre / sed / sueño.	I am (not) hungry / thirsty / tired.
tiempo para cocinar	time to cook
contiene / contienen	it contains / they contain
La fibra …	Fibre …
protege contra el cáncer	protects against cancer
combate la obesidad	combats obesity
reduce el riesgo de enfermedades	reduces the risk of diseases
evitar comer / beber	avoid eating / drinking
cambiar mi dieta	change my diet
llevar una dieta equilibrada	have a balanced diet
preparar con ingredientes frescos	prepare with fresh ingredients
engordar	to put on weight
saltarse el desayuno	to skip breakfast
practicar más deporte	to do more sport

Had a look ☐ Nearly there ☐ Nailed it ☐

M8

Módulo 8 Palabras

¡Vivir a tope!
Beber alcohol …	Drinking alcohol …
Fumar cigarrillos / porros …	To smoke / Smoking cigarettes / joints …
Tomar drogas blandas / duras …	To take / Taking soft / hard drugs …
Es / No es …	It is / isn't …
ilegal / peligroso	illegal / dangerous
un malgasto de dinero	a waste of money
una tontería / un problema serio	stupid / a serious problem
un vicio muy caro	an expensive habit
muy perjudicial para la salud	very damaging to your health
tan malo	as bad
provoca mal aliento	causes bad breath
daña los pulmones	damages the lungs
mancha los dientes de amarillo	stains your teeth yellow
causa el fracaso escolar / depresión	causes failure at school / depression
produce una fuerte dependencia física	produces a strong, physical dependence
tiene muchos riesgos	has many risks
afecta a tu capacidad para tomar decisiones	affects your capacity to make decisions
te relaja / te quita el estrés	relaxes you / relieves stress
te quita el sueño / control	robs you of sleep / self-control
te hace sentir bien / más adulto	makes you feel good / more adult

Had a look ☐ Nearly there ☐ Nailed it ☐

Es fácil engancharse.	It's easy to get hooked.
¡Qué asco!	How disgusting!
Cedí ante la presión de grupo.	I gave in to peer pressure.
Caí en el hábito de …	I fell into the habit of …
Empecé a …	I started to …
Perdí peso.	I lost weight.
No puedo parar.	I can't stop.
Ya he empezado a …	I've already started to …
Todavía no he dejado de …	I still haven't given up …
A partir de ahora intentaré …	From now on I will try to …

Had a look ☐ Nearly there ☐ Nailed it ☐

¡El deporte nos une!
¿Para qué sirven …?	What are …for?
los eventos deportivos internacionales	international sporting events
los grandes acontecimientos deportivos	big sporting events
los Juegos Paralímpicos / Olímpicos	the Paralympics / Olympics
la Copa Mundial del Fútbol	the Football World Cup
Sirven para …	They serve to …
promover …	promote / foster / encourage …
la participación en el deporte	participation in sport
el espíritu de solidaridad	team spirit
regenerar los centros urbanos	regenerate city centres
elevar el orgullo nacional	increase national pride
transmitir los valores de respeto y disciplina	convey / instil the values of respect and discipline
unir a la gente	unite people
dar un impulso económico	give a boost to the economy
inspirar a la gente	inspire people

Had a look ☐ Nearly there ☐ Nailed it ☐

Una / Otra desventaja es …	A / Another disadvantage is …
el riesgo de ataques terroristas	the risk of terrorist attacks
el tráfico	the traffic
el dopaje	doping
la deuda	the debt
el coste de organización de la seguridad	the cost of organising the security
la ciudad anfitriona	the host city
el voluntariado	volunteering
Solicité un trabajo voluntario porque …	I applied for a volunteering job because …
(Nunca) Había sido …	I had (never) been …
Antes ya había trabajado como …	Previously I had already worked as …

Had a look ☐ Nearly there ☐ Nailed it ☐

¡Apúntate!
¿Qué estabas haciendo?	What were you doing?
Estaba / Estábamos / Estaban …	I/He/She/It was / We were / They were …
ensayando	rehearsing
nevando	snowing
entrando en casa	coming into the house
durmiendo	sleeping
conduciendo por la ciudad	driving through the city
leyendo	reading
volando por el aire	flying through the air
Se estaba convirtiendo en un río.	It was turning into a river.
Se estaba moviendo.	It was moving.
a mi alrededor	around me
Se estaban cayendo.	They were falling.
¿Cómo te enteraste del/ de la/de las …?	How did you find out about the …?
temblor	tremor

Módulo 8 Palabras

incendio forestal	*forest fire*
huracán	*hurricane*
tornado	*tornado*
terremoto	*earthquake*
tormenta de nieve	*snow storm*
acción humanitaria	*humanitarian campaign*
inundaciones	*floods*

Had a look ☐ **Nearly there** ☐ **Nailed it** ☐

Estaba …	*He/She was …*
mirando / viendo las noticias / la tele	*watching the news / the TV*
buscando informaciones en línea	*looking for information online*
charlando con un amigo / una amiga	*chatting with a friend*
leyendo un post en Facebook	*reading a Facebook post*
cuando …	*when …*
encontré un reportaje / un artículo	*I found a report / an article*
recibí un SMS	*I received a text message*
(lo) vi en las noticias	*I saw (it) on the news*
mi novio me llamó / me contó la historia	*my boyfriend called me / told me the story*

Had a look ☐ **Nearly there** ☐ **Nailed it** ☐

una organización de servicio voluntario	*a voluntary organisation*
una campaña para las víctimas	*a campaign for the victims*
una caja de supervivencia	*a survival box*
Decidí apuntarme.	*I decided to sign up.*
recaudar fondos / solicitar donativos	*to raise funds / to ask for donations*
organizamos algunos eventos	*we organised some events*
un concierto / un espectáculo de baile	*a concert / a dance show*
una carrera de bici apadrinada	*a sponsored bike race*
una venta de pasteles	*a cake sale*
ser solidario	*showing solidarity / supporting*
Te hace sentir más conectado con los demás.	*It makes you feed more connected to others.*

Had a look ☐ **Nearly there** ☐ **Nailed it** ☐

M 8

Módulo 8 Palabras

Extra words I should know for reading and listening activities

Verbos útiles	*Useful verbs*
afiliarse a un club	to join a club
aprovechar una experiencia previa	to make the most of a previous experience
asomarse por la ventana	to look out of a window
colaborar en un evento	to take part in an event
conseguir hacer algo	to manage to do something
crear conciencia	to raise consciousness
darse cuenta	to realise
dedicar tiempo	to spend time
dejar de fumar / beber / tomar drogas	to give up smoking / drinking / taking drugs
demostrar	to demonstrate
desarrollar	to develop
destruir (la selva)	to destroy (the rainforest)
emborracharse	to get drunk

Had a look ☐ **Nearly there** ☐ **Nailed it** ☐

fomentar el espíritu de solidaridad	to promote a spirit of solidarity
frenar	to stop / to break
hacer una revisión de algo	to check something (over)
instalarse	to settle
ir de carreras	to race
llevarse (algo) a la tumba	to take (something) to the grave
mantenerse en forma	to keep fit
Me queda mucho por hacer.	I've got a long way to go. / I've still got a lot to do.
ocuparse de	to be in charge of
provocar molestias	to cause annoyance
quitar la vida a alguien	to cause someone to die
recoger	to collect
tener para comer	to have enough to eat

Had a look ☐ **Nearly there** ☐ **Nailed it** ☐

⭐ ***How to spot opposites***
In English 'un-' is often used before an adjective to give the opposite, for example: forgettable → **un**forgettable. In Spanish *in*- is used in the same way, for example: *olvidable* (you may already know that *olvidar* means 'to forget') → **in**olvidable. Some other examples are:
capaz → **in**capaz
eficiente → **in**eficiente
feliz → **in**feliz
justo → **in**justo
See if you can think of some more. You could use a dictionary to help you.

Nombres útiles	*Useful nouns*
el agua potable	drinking water
el banco de alimentos	food bank
la caminata patrocinada	sponsored walk
el/la compatriota	fellow countryman / countrywoman
la confianza en sí mismo/a	self-confidence
el entorno	surrounding area
la escasez	shortage / scarcity
una experiencia inolvidable*	an unforgettable experience
la falta (de algo)	the lack (of something)
los hidratos de carbono	carbohydrates
jóvenes y jubilados	young and old
los Juegos Olímpicos (JJ. OO.)	Olympic Games
los países en desarrollo	developing countries

Had a look ☐ **Nearly there** ☐ **Nailed it** ☐

el piso**	flat / floor
la planta baja	ground floor
el recorrido	the route (of a race)
el/la refugiado/a	refugee
la revuelta	uprising
la risa	laugh
el saneamiento	sanitation
el seísmo / terremoto	earthquake
la sociedad de usar y tirar	throwaway society
el sótano	basement
el sufrimiento	suffering
la supervivencia	survival
el voluntariado	voluntary work

Had a look ☐ **Nearly there** ☐ **Nailed it** ☐

Otras palabras útiles	*Other useful words*
aconsejable	advisable
adecuado/a	adequate
amueblado/a	furnished
disponible	available
en ruta hacia	on the way to
oscuro/a	dark
reciclado/a	recyled
sin techo	homeless
subterráneo/a	underground

Had a look ☐ **Nearly there** ☐ **Nailed it** ☐

⭐ ****Watch and listen out for words that have more than one meaning***
Be aware that *el piso* can mean 'flat' or 'floor' depending on context. So, for example, *Vivo en el primer / tercer piso* means 'I live on the first / third floor', but *Vivo en un piso con cuatro habitaciones* means 'I live in a flat / apartment with four rooms'.